A HISTORY OF
FLORIDA FORTS

A HISTORY OF FLORIDA FORTS
FLORIDA'S LONELY OUTPOSTS

ALEJANDRO M. DE QUESADA

THE
History
PRESS

Published by The History Press
Charleston, SC 29403
www.historypress.net

Cover photo: Battery Charles Mellon, Fort Dade, as it appears today.
All images courtesy of AdeQ Archives unless otherwise noted.

First published 2006
Second printing 2010
Third printing 2012
Fourth printing 2013

ISBN 978.1.54020.400.4

Library of Congress Cataloging-in-Publication Data

De Quesada, A. M.
A history of Florida forts : Florida's lonely outposts / Alejandro M. de
Quesada Jr.
p. cm.
Includes bibliographical references.
ISBN 978.1-59629-104-1 (alk. paper)
1. Fortification--Florida--History. 2. Florida--History, Local. 3.
Florida--History, Military. I. Title.
F312.D4 2006
975.9--dc22
2006013231

Contents

CONTENTS

Acknowledgements

I would like to thank the following individuals and organizations that have contributed information and materials to make this book possible. They are: Ron Hickox, former curator of the Hillsborough County Veterans Memorial Museum and Park; Bruce Graetz, Museum of Florida History; Bettie, Earl and Jeremy DeBary, Marion County Museum of History; Bob Baker, Egmont Key State Park; Katie Roberson, San Marcos de Apalache State Historic Site; Andrea White, Bureau of Archaeological Research; Richard L. Ehrlich, PhD, Mission San Luis; St. Petersburg Historical Society; Paul Camps, Special Collections, University of South Florida; Hal Hubner, Special Collections librarian, Lakeland Public Library; Anita McNutt, Heritage Tourism, City of St. Augustine; Southwest Florida Museum of History; Cedar Key Historical Society; Fort Myers Historical Society; Fort Lauderdale Historical Society; Vincent Luisi, Dunedin Historical Museum; Key West Art & Historical Society; Hillsborough County Historical Commission; Pinellas County Historical Commission; Florida Historical Society; Tampa Historical Society; Pensacola Historical Society; The Company of Military Historians; Coast Defense Study Group; Council on Abandoned Military Posts; all the parks and historic sites within the National Park Service: Fort Barrancas, Fort Caroline, Castillo de San Marcos, Fort Matanzas, Fort Jefferson and Fort Pickens; all the historic sites under the Florida Division of Historical Resources and Division of Recreation and Parks: Addison Blockhouse State Historic Site & Tomoka State Park, Bulow Plantation Ruins; Dade Battlefield State Historic Site, Ceder Key State Museum, Colonial Spanish Quarter, Fort Clinch, Fort Cooper, Fort Dade (Egmont Key), Fort Foster, Fort Gadsden, Fort Mose, Fort San Carlos, Fort San Marcos de Apalache, Fort Zachary Taylor and Paynes Creek State Historic Site; Fort DeSoto, Pinellas County Parks and Recreation; Fort Christmas, Orange County Parks Department; Fort Conde, Mobile Chamber of Commerce. Finally, I would like to give thanks to my daughter, Caroline de Quesada, who's been a part of my twenty-five years of research and shared in my fascination with Florida's fortified past.

Introduction

When I started my research on the forts that had existed on the Florida peninsula, I found out that nothing much had been written about them as a whole. Florida often has been called the country's most fortified state, with more than three hundred camps, batteries, forts and redoubts that existed from the earliest settlement to the present. So through this work I'll present some of the well-known and not-so-well-known forts that affected the history of our state.

According to James Gray's *Florida Forts*, fortification in Florida began in three main stages of its history: those from the colonial period, those of the Seminole Wars and those that were constructed before and after the Civil War.

In colonial Florida, forts were primitive, simple and hastily built. Almost all were of earth, with or without supporting timber, though in certain of them a degree of durability was achieved by erecting parallel stone or brick walls twelve or fifteen feet apart and packing the intermediate space with earth or sand. Often in the seventeenth- and eighteenth-century works, forts were bastioned, a concept started in Italy about 1450. But the early earthwork defenses were often temporarily used and abandoned to decay, although a strategic point at a harbor or river opening might be intermittently occupied and abandoned, thus serving as the site for a succession of works, according to Lewis's *Seacoast Fortifications of the United States*.

There were some exceptions to the trend of constructing defensive works in colonial times. The majority of them were mainly constructed of wood and earth and fell victim to fire, humid climates and shoddy construction. The Castillo de San Marcos was an example of the need for permanent fortifications. Though indeed some permanent fortifications were made out of bricks or stones, the Castillo is unique in that it was totally constructed out of shell stones called coquina, which has a durability and resistance to cannon fire. Another fort, the Battery San Antonio, consisted of earth, brick and stucco. Located in the Pensacola area, this fort is probably one of the few in Florida that marks the variety in Spanish military architecture in existence today.

The armaments used to protect these colonial forts were often of light calibers—from the smallest to sixteen-pounder, eighteen-pounder and twenty-four-pounder. In some permanent works the largest would be forty-pounders (the cannons that fired only solid, spherical shot were expressed by the weight of the shot determining its caliber). The cannons were usually supported by carriages similar to those used in naval ships. In the years before and after the American Revolution, the forts in Florida fell to disrepair and decay under the British and Spanish occupations. When the United States acquired the territory of Florida from Spain in 1821, a large number of forts remained in existence; but most of them were simply in shambles. Thus, an effort was made to refortify Florida all over again.

In the Seminole Wars of 1817–18 and 1835–42, the state of Florida became overabundant with more than eighty blockhouses, camps, forts and stockades. During these wars, the forts were found throughout Florida from the south of Apalachicola to every part of the peninsula. Virtually all American forts of the Seminole Wars were simple defensive works, usually a combination of ditches and embankments of earth and trees to protect relatively small military units for short periods of time. Their temporary nature means that traces of them have disappeared, as Morris reports in *Florida Place Names*.

The Seminole Wars brought things that were often overlooked. For the first time the interior was explored and mapped. The army laid out many trails and roads, writes Tebeau in *A History of Florida*. The large number of forts soon became clustered with settlements that survive today under the names of the fort or the ones named by the early settlers. Today some communities still retain the names of the forts: Fort Basinger, Fort Lauderdale, Fort Meade, Fort Myers, Fort Pierce, Fort Walton and Fort White. Though many communities were named after forts, some have eliminated the "Fort" from their names: Dade City was once Fort Dade, Denaud was once Fort Denaud, Jupiter was once Fort Jupiter and Maitland was once Fort Maitland. And yet others are known now by different names: Bartow was Fort Blount, Clearwater was Fort Harrison, Miami was Fort Dallas, Tampa was once Fort Brooke and so on.

The basic armament for these frontier outposts was the musket. Due to their temporary nature and locations some of these forts did not have cannons, but those that did carried either six- and twelve-pounder guns, a twelve-pounder field howitzer or twenty-four- and thirty-two-pounder howitzers, all of which were of War of 1812 and Mexican War vintage. There was also a Third Seminole War in 1855–58, which only led to reactivation of some of the old forts and construction of new ones southeastward form Fort Harvie (renamed Fort Myers) on the Caloosahatchee River. In terms of lives lost and money expended, the Seminole Wars (especially the Second Seminole War) were the costliest of American Indian War expeditions, according to Eden's *Fort Cooper—April 1836*.

The great masonry forts that were built preceding the Civil War are found in a variety of forms. These forts were known as third systems that came from the drawing boards of the Bernard Board, headed by Simon Bernard, who served as a general under Napoleon. Their main purpose was to replace the earlier works guarding the seacoasts.

These systems of forts were designed to deal with invasion from the sea and wooden warships. Fitzgerald and Hinds write in *Bulwark and Bastion* that all these works generally have two or three tiers of vaulted gunrooms or bombproof casemates, in addition to gun positions on the ramparts. One feature that was added to these forts was protection for the gunners within the casemates. This feature found in these works was provided with iron embrasure shutters two inches thick, which opened the moment a piece was fired, then slammed shut to shield the gun and its crew from grape shot and sharpshooters during preparations for the following round, as Lewis explains. This innovation was thought out by a world figure in seacoast fortification, Joseph G. Totten, and was to become internationally known as the Totten embrasure.

In the years preceding and a short while after the Civil War there were two general types of guns used. The barbette carriage gun generally fired over the parapet wall. The gun fired from a casemate was housed in a small chamber directly behind the wall and fired through a slit or loophole in the wall, writes Burns in *Confederate Forts*. The guns that fired from barbette carriages from the parapet walls and from casemates were usually thirty-two- and forty-two-pounder iron seacoast guns, with twenty-four-pounder bronze howitzers that sometimes lay in the bastions to flank the long reaches of the fort walls. During the Civil War the barbette carriage was replaced from the parapet walls by big guns such as Columbiads and Rodmans. But with the introduction of rifled guns and their effectiveness in the destruction of masonry forts such as Fort Pulaski in Georgia, the need for better fortifications was realized.

After the Civil War these forts were considered obsolete for defense, but though considered outdated, these forts continued to serve, out of necessity, as a main source of defense. By 1890 these forts were still armed with smoothbore guns of Civil War vintage, with some Rodmans that remained in service until after 1900. Also around 1885 some ten-inch Rodmans were converted into eight-inch muzzle-loading rifles by sleeve insertions, as a means of updating them. In the years after termination of constructing forts in the mid-1870s, and with older works falling into disrepair, defense for the state of Florida and the rest of the country probably reached its lowest point since the War of 1812.

In the post-war years, several new developments in military weapons completely changed the defense of the nation's seacoasts. One was the change from black powder to nitroglycerin-based propellants; also, guns could be built to load from the rear (breech) instead of the front (muzzle) as reported in "Concrete Batteries—The Endicott System." This made defense more efficient and enabled guns to fire faster, at greater distances and with pinpoint accuracy.

In 1885 President Grover Cleveland appointed a special board, headed by War Secretary William C. Endicott, to review the nation's entire coastal defense and to make recommendations for a defense system using the new technology. Construction of the Endicott System began in the 1890s and continued toward the Second World War with plans to fortify more than twenty-six coastal locations. In this period, the harbors of the United States once again came to be protected by a vast body of fortifications, almost all

The author began his fascination and research on Florida's forts when he was a freshman in high school; over twenty-five years later he is still uncovering new information and discovering lost fort sites. He is seen here with his daughter, Caroline, on one of their many historical trips around the state over the years.

of which, except for their armament, remain in existence today, writes Lewis. The new fortifications were made out of reinforced concrete, simple in form and designed to blend as closely as possible into the surrounding landscape. The insistence upon the concrete fortifications was for the guns and their carriages, which were far more complex than their older counterparts.

The major armament of the Endicott era consisted of six-, eight-, ten- and twelve-inch caliber guns; all fired projectiles weighing up to half a ton, which were mechanically hoisted up to them (the ammunition magazines were located nearby to the gun emplacements, at a level several feet lower, and roofed by about twelve feet of reinforced concrete). The majority of the guns were mounted on disappearing carriages that could be lowered for loading and allowed concealment and protection from enemy fire until raised for the next shot. They were mounted in massive emplacements whose edges were at ground level and its concrete walls were made to be about twenty feet thick behind thirty or more feet of earth. From the sea these emplacements were almost invisible and impregnable from attack. Also the defenses included large numbers of mortars and light-caliber rapid-fire guns.

During each successive war (the Spanish-American War and both World Wars) troops have manned the various guns in the batteries found in our state. But the technology of World War II made the Endicott system obsolete and the batteries were soon abandoned. Today you can find heavy concentrations of these batteries in the Pensacola and Tampa areas; many of these are now preserved as monuments to a bygone era. But a few remain ignored and fated to a state of disrepair and oblivion, such as Fort Dade on Egmont Key in Tampa Bay.

This work deals with some forts that have been forgotten and some that have been remembered for their role in our state's history, for they are Florida's lonely outposts.

Chapter One

THE COLONIAL ERA

CASTILLO DE SAN MARCOS AND THE DEFENSES OF ST. AUGUSTINE

In 1565 St. Augustine was founded by Pedro Menéndez de Avilés in response to French encroachment into Spanish Florida. A series of wooden fortifications were built, but they were not sufficient in preventing attacks by foreign military forces and pirates. An English fleet with two thousand men under the command of Sir Francis Drake landed in, sacked and burned St. Augustine in June 1586. In 1668 two Spanish supply ships sailed quietly into the harbor of St. Augustine. The ships had actually been captured earlier by pirates under the command of John Davis and were used as a "Trojan Horse" of sorts. At night the pirates landed and took the town by surprise. The fort withstood the attack; however, the town was plundered. Sixty Spaniards were killed. These events, followed by the English settlement of Charles Towne in 1670, caused the Spanish crown to consider a superior defensive fortification to be built in St. Augustine.

In 1672 construction began on the Castillo de San Marcos and work continued at intervals until 1695. The new fort was to replace the ninth of a series of wooden forts that had defended St. Augustine since 1565. The stone for the fort, a shell-rock called coquina, was quarried on nearby Anastasia Island. In 1683 pirates overtook the small Spanish detachment at the watchtower in Matanzas, but one soldier was able to escape and warn the garrison in the town. The pirates were ambushed by the Spaniards, who forced the pirates back to their ship. Another pirate raid was repulsed in 1686 at Little Matanzas Inlet.

The Castillo de San Marcos's baptism by fire came when British forces under Governor James Moore of Carolina besieged the fort in 1702. The fort's guns kept the British at bay and after a two-month siege, a Spanish fleet appeared and Moore was forced to retreat overland after burning the town and his own ships. A second attack upon St. Augustine by Colonel Palmer of Carolina was repulsed in 1728.General James Oglethorpe led an expedition of one thousand men against St. Augustine in June 1740. A twenty-seven-day bombardment of St. Augustine and the Castillo de San Marcos ensued. After some victorious raids on British-held positions by Spanish troops and Spanish supply ships arriving from Havana, Oglethorpe was forced to end his siege after thirty-eight days. In 1742 a stone tower was completed at Matanzas as well as two additional defensive lines to the north of the Castillo.

In 1763 Spain ceded Florida to Great Britain in return for British-occupied Havana. The British strengthened the Castillo and the town's defenses. During the American Revolution the Castillo became a base for British military operations against Georgia and South Carolina. Three signers of the Declaration of Independence were interned at the fort. With Galvez's victory in Pensacola and the Treaty of Paris of 1783, Florida was once again returned to Spain. In 1821 Spain ceded Florida to the United States after years of small uprisings and rebellions such as "Florida's French Revolution."

With St. Augustine now in American hands, the Castillo de San Marcos was renamed Fort Marion. Throughout the nineteenth century the fort served as a military prison during the Second Seminole, Civil and Spanish-American Wars. It was briefly held by Confederate troops during the War Between the States. In 1924 Fort Marion became a national monument by presidential proclamation, and in 1942 the fort was renamed Castillo de San Marcos.

Following the 1702 siege by the British, the Spanish began construction of a system of peripheral fortifications to protect the town based on the principle of defense-in-depth. Between 1704 and 1821 the Spanish completed the outworks of the Castillo and erected five earthen walls known as lines of entrenchment. The Rosario Line and the eastern segment of the Cubo Line formed the city wall, also known as the line of circumvallation. In the 1730s the line was rebuilt in anticipation of another English attack from the north. During the British occupation of Florida (1763–84), military engineers repaired the Spanish fortifications and erected a chain of seven free-standing redoubts west and south of the town. The existing Spanish redoubts of the Cubo Line were renamed, such as the Santo Domingo Redoubt, also known as the Tolomato Redoubt, which was renamed Fort Moultrie.

In 1808 the Santo Domingo Redoubt was again rebuilt to strengthen St. Augustine's defenses. The four embrasures pierced the walls of the redoubt to accommodate ordnance pieces, typically four-, six- and eight-pounder guns mounted on siege and field carriages. In the absence of field pieces, garrison guns from the Castillo were moved to the redoubt. In 1834, on the eve of the Second Seminole War (1835–42), the U.S. Army constructed a wooden redoubt on the site of the ruined Santo Domingo Redoubt. Today, reconstructions of the 1808 Santo Domingo Redoubt stand again on Cordova and Orange Streets and the Cubo Line extending from the Castillo de San Marcos. The City Gate and the outline of the defenses along Cordova Street are the only original vestiges of the Cubo Line.

A series of wooden forts was built between St. Augustine's founding in 1565 and 1672, like the one shown here at Ponce de Leon's Fountain of Youth Archeological Park.

The site of the original fort of St. Augustine is located within the grounds of Ponce de Leon's Fountain of Youth Archeological Park.

Construction began on the great stone fortification of Castillo de San Marcos in 1672. *Courtesy of National Park Service.*

The Castillo was renamed Fort Marion when the U.S. took possession of the fort in 1821. Union soldiers are seen upon the ramparts during the Civil War.

Ordnance and materials are seen stored in the fort's parade ground. Note that every valuable space for quarters has been utilized by these Union soldiers, as evidenced by the tents on the ramparts.

Throughout the American military occupation of the fort it still retained much of its characteristic Spanish architectural style.

In the years following the Civil War the fort came under caretaker status.

The fort became a national monument in 1924 and was renamed Castillo de San Marcos.

The Castillo's courtyard, showing the entrance to the chapel.

The enlisted quarters for the Spanish garrison were spartan.

The Cubo Line extended from the Castillo and formed part of the town's defenses.

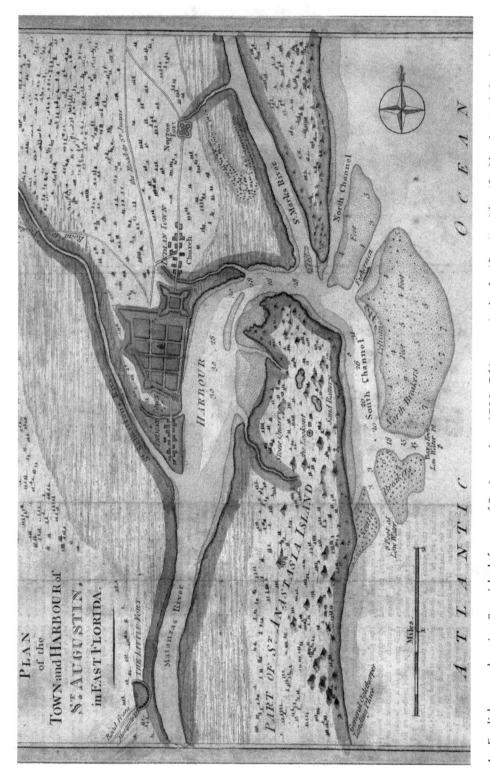

An English map showing Spanish defenses of St. Augustine, 1780. Of interest is the fortification identified by the English as the Negroe Fort, which was Fort Mose, seen in the middle-right portion of the map.

Next to the Castillo, the town's gate is the only original fragment remaining of the city's early defenses.

A reconstruction of the Santo Domingo Redoubt stands on Cordova and Orange Streets.

Another part of St. Augustine's defenses was the fortified lighthouse on Anastasia Island. It disappeared due to beach erosion in the latter half of the nineteenth century. *Courtesy of Florida State Archives.*

Bateria de San Antonio

There are few reminders of the Spanish presence in West Florida. One of these would be the Bateria de San Antonio, which was part of the many Spanish and English fortifications that were found all over Pensacola. Previous fortifications had protected the hill of Barrancas in which the present structure of the Spanish battery now stands. During the British period of occupation in both East and West Florida, from 1763 to 1783, a fortification was built on the Barrancas in 1771 and was known as the Royal Navy Redoubt. When Spain formally regained Florida in 1783, the former British fort was renamed Fort San Carlos de Barrancas.

The newly acquired fort on Barrancas wasn't sufficient for protection of Pensacola Bay. When Spain declared war on England in October of 1796, plans for a more permanent fortification in the area were discussed by a Council of War in Spanish New Orleans. The

Bateria de San Antonio de Barrancas, Pensacola.

Royal Navy Redoubt was not capable of stopping Galvez's invasion force in 1781 and the Spaniards would not want the same episode to happen to them. The fortification was to be a seven-gun masonry water battery or medialuna and was to be located at the foot of the hill of Barrancas. Its guns would have a better coverage of the bay's entrance than the former British fort atop the same hill by delivering ricochet fire over the surface of the bay to hit ships at the waterline. Construction began under the direction of Francisco P. Gelabert in 1797.

By 1798, the battery was nearly completed when the Spanish realized that the new fortification had no means of protecting itself from the rear. The former British fort on top of the hill, now renamed San Carlos de Barrancas, had fallen into disuse. In 1821 Florida was ceded to the United States and U.S. Army Engineers found the masonry fort usable when it was repaired in 1840. The next history of the battery continues on with the construction of Fort Barrancas in the 1840s.

The Bateria de San Antonio's magazine showing typical Spanish decor.

Aerial view of the Bateria de San Antonio de Barrancas and later Civil War–era fortification known as Fort Barrancas. *Courtesy of National Park Service.*

A History of Florida Forts

Fort Caroline

Despite the fact that it was Spain who had discovered Florida and claimed it by Ponce de Leon in 1513, it was the French who started the first settlement in Florida in 1564. These Huguenot Frenchmen would be hailed by some as the first Protestant settlers in the New World. To Spain, these French "heretics" would merely be considered trespassers in Spanish territory and would probably pose a threat to Spanish shipping in the Atlantic. The intrusion would force Spain's hand in what needed to be done with the French and the status of the territory of Florida. This begins the tragic short history of the French settlement of Fort Caroline.

A small expedition under the command of Jean Jacques Ribault and Rene de Laudonniere had arrived in the St. Johns River area in search of a suitable site for settlement around May 1562. These French Huguenots, recognized by John Calvin and Charles IX of France, were seeking refuge from religious persecution that was prevalent in Europe during the sixteenth century. When the French explorers found the area to be satisfactory, these Huguenots proceeded to give their first Protestant service in the New World and at the mouth of the river a monument was constructed to declare the French claim in the area. These men then continued on to an area near Port Royal, in South Carolina, and constructed another monument to declare their presence. Before returning to France, Ribault decided to leave a small garrison of men to remain there temporarily, to protect their recently acquired claims. Two years would elapse before these French Huguenots would return to Florida.

After many delays, Laudonniere's group of three hundred men and women arrived at the St. Johns River, then called the River of May, on June 24, 1564. The following day the settlers selected the site for a fort upon a bluff and named it Fort Caroline, after Charles IX of France. The site was selected for its commanding view and its future use as a productive farmland. Ribault's view of the land was that "the sight of the faire meadowes is a pleasure not able to be expressed with tongue" and even Laudonniere had stated that "the place was so pleasant that melancholias would be forced to change their nature," writes Bennett in "Fort Caroline, Cradle of American Freedom."

The triangular fort was built in the European manner, which was quite different from the square frontier forts of the Second Seminole War in the early nineteenth century. The two corners of the fort facing the river formed a nine-foot battlement consisting of earth supported by logs. The fort's apex faced south and a moat was constructed, in which the waters from the St. Johns River would surround all sides of the fort. On the western side of the fort were located the gate and bridge. Over the gate stood the French coat of arms and the family crest of Admiral Gaspard Coligny, the colony's financial backer. Within the fort, buildings were constructed to store weapons and ammunition and a few for habitation as well. It appears that the fort soon became overcrowded and that a few of the colonists built shacks for themselves outside the confines of the fort.

Conditions at Fort Caroline went well at first; however, the colonists began to have trouble raising crops in the Florida climate. They relied primarily on the animals they had brought with them from France for food: dogs, sheep, mules, chickens, horses, pigs and some cattle. Soon malaria had spread into the safety of the fort. Talk of abandoning the colony was prevalent amongst the colonists. However, the discouraging talks subsided when the pirate Sir John Hawkins paid a visit to the French colony in 1565. The English buccaneer, while playing a cat-and-mouse game with the Spanish Navy, had arrived at the mouth of the river in search of fresh water. Laudonniere's colonists traded their only cannon for badly needed food and clothing. After a short rest, the pirate captain and crew sailed away to resume plundering and harassing the Spanish silver and gold fleet. Within a month, the colonists were also prepared to abandon Fort Caroline when Jean Ribault arrived with reinforcements.

On August 28, 1565, Ribault's reinforcement of six hundred men and women arrived to relieve the hapless colonists at Fort Caroline. On that same day when Ribault had reached the mouth of the St. Johns River, a Spanish force under the command of Pedro Menendez de Aviles was approaching the coast of Florida. Since the discovery of the territory by Juan Ponce de Leon in 1513 the Spaniards had claimed Florida. King Philip II of Spain decided that the French Protestants must be driven out from Florida and that the territory be held and maintained by a permanent garrison at various strategic locations. This hatred of the Protestants by Catholics, and vice versa, was an outgrowth of the Reformation and Counter-Reformation that plagued Europe with violence during the sixteenth century and the following three centuries thereafter.

The Spanish force had settled upon Anastasia Island and began to fortify the area. These fortifications would mark the beginning of St. Augustine, the oldest surviving and living settlement in North America. There were previous Spanish attempts in establishing a settlement in Florida. To name one attempt, an Aragonese nobleman, Tristan de Luna y Arellano, was ordered to depart Veracruz and to establish a settlement in Ochuse, now present-day Pensacola. The Spaniards arrived at the site on August 14, 1559, but after many hardships the site was abandoned nearly two years later. However, the French presence had threatened Spanish hegemony in the area. Soon, five of Menendez's ships had encountered four French ships, in which the French escaped into the open sea. The Spaniards found out the location of Fort Caroline from the local Indian population and made preparations for an attack. The French Huguenots made plans for attack upon the Spaniards as well.

The French plan was to attack the Spaniards by sea, while the Spaniards planned to attack by land. Ribault and every man able to carry a weapon were boarded into the French ships and headed south toward the Spanish encampment. But, upon sight of the Spanish forces, a tropical storm swept Ribault's ships farther south, approximately toward present-day Daytona Beach and Cape Canaveral. With a contingent of five hundred soldiers, Menendez marched toward Fort Caroline and encamped at a pond near the fort on September 19, 1565. After a council of war, Menendez decided to attack despite dissension amongst some of his officers and men. In the early morning of September 20, the Spaniards rushed into the fort with hardly any resistance from the small number of soldiers that Ribault had left behind to defend.

The events that occurred soon afterward become sketchy and the intentions of Menendez become highly questionable. When the first wave of Spanish troops stormed into the fort, they found sacrilegious articles that would have earned the French a massacre: "Many packs of playing cards with the figure of the Host and Chalice on the backs, and many saints with crosses on their shoulders and other playing cards burlesquing things of the Church," reported Jahoda in *Florida: A History*. Close to 140 men, women and children were indiscriminately slaughtered by the Spanish soldiers. This number included two of Hawkins's sailors who were left behind by the infamous pirate. During the melee, "some infants were killed and their bodies erected on the points of pikes stuck in the ground," according to Bennett's "Fort Caroline, Cradle of American Freedom." It appeared that Menendez was in the rear guard when he arrived at the fort; by then the slaughters were already being commenced by the advance troops. The Spaniard shouted once he entered the fort's compound, "in a loud voice that no woman, nor boy under fifteen years of age, should be killed, by which 70 were saved," records Davis in "Fort Caroline." There were no Spanish losses at the battle for Fort Caroline.

There were few survivors that managed to escape the massacare and capture by the Spaniards. The ones that were able to scale over the fort's walls and those that feigned death were able to escape to the nearby French ships that were left behind by Ribault. One of those that had made it to the safety of the French ship was Laudonniere himself. He was left behind due to an illness and was wounded when the Spaniards made their attack upon the fort. The French survivors reported that the Spaniards took "the eyes of the dead and flicked them from the points of their daggers in the direction of the French boats," writes Bennett in "Fort Caroline, Cradle of American Freedom." The survivors managed to sail for France and arrived there without any problems. Also, a few other survivors managed to find protection from their Indian allies.

Meanwhile, nearly all of Ribault's men made it to the shore after their ships wrecked along the Florida coast, south of Anastasia Island. The Frenchmen decided to march back to Fort Caroline, not knowing the fate of their comrades and families. Menendez departed the former French fort, now renamed as Fort San Mateo, and was informed by Indians that the French were in the vicinity of an inlet near St. Augustine. Menendez wasted no time in getting to the inlet. After promising mercy to a group of French Huguenots, Menendez ordered groups of ten French prisoners to be tied together and led off to certain areas of the inlet to be put to the sword. Another group with Ribault met the same fate as the others several days later, on that same inlet. The blood of over three hundred French Huguenots was spilled on the sandy inlet, now called Matanzas or Slaughter Inlet. Those who were spared were the ones who declared themselves as Catholics and those who would be useful as artisans or workmen.

Some early accounts mentioned that to confirm the death of Ribault and to remind what the penalty would be for those who strayed away from the Spanish crown and church, "Ribault's beard and skin were sent to King Philip of Spain and his head was cut in four pieces, which were distributed on the ends of lances on each corner of the fort at St. Augustine," writes Bennett in "Fort Caroline, Cradle of American Freedom." Spain had made its bloody statement that Spanish territories would be protected and defended. This battle was the first that involved an international conflict between European nations upon this North American continent.

Many of those who were captured remained in St. Augustine for the next few years. These French were given better treatment, for the short war was brief and expedient. A few of the French captives were sent to Havana, Cuba, when Menendez, appointed as royal governor of Florida, sailed for the island for supplies. In a letter to the king from Menendez, dated October 15, 1565, among the captives that were brought to St. Augustine was a boy that was born at the former French fort. "Here we have a record of the first white child of Protestant parentage born in North America—more than twenty years before the birth of Virginia Dare," reports Davis in "Fort Caroline."

At the former Fort Caroline on St. Johns Bluff, the French coat of arms was replaced with that of Spain. The fort's name was changed to Fort San Mateo and the Spaniards also changed the river's name from the River of May to the St. Johns (San Juan) River. The fort continued to be used as an outpost and as a mission. However, the Spanish garrison was continually harassed by Timuquan Indians who were friendly to the French colonists. By May 1566, both forts in St. Augustine and San Mateo were reinforced by an armada of fourteen ships and fifteen hundred men. These were sent by the Spanish king in order to prevent a French invasion of Florida. Close to three years after the massacare at Fort Caroline and on Matanzas Inlet, the French would have their day of revenge.

Around Easter 1568, a French expedition under the command of Dominique de Gourgues arrived at the mouth of the St. Johns River. Their goal was to avenge the slaughter of their countrymen. The French attacked Fort San Mateo and massacred most of the four hundred men of the Spanish garrison. The French, also with the aid of some of their Timuquan Indian allies, killed or hanged every Spaniard that fell into their hands. When Menendez had tacked up a sign over the bodies of the hanged Huguenots at the fort, it read that the action was not done "unto Frenchmen but unto heretics." In response, the French also tacked a sign over the hanged bodies of the Spaniards, stating that the French act was not done unto "Spaniards, but as to robbers and murderers," according to Bennett's "Fort Caroline, Cradle of American Freedom." A full cycle had been made with this sequence of events.

Despite the tragic events that took place at the former French fort, San Mateo continued to survive and serve its function as an outpost. When Sir Francis Drake, the well-known English pirate, pillaged and burned St. Augustine, most of the Spanish inhabitants had found refuge in Fort San Mateo in 1586. Within a century, the fort would gradually fade away into the pages of history. However, the fort's site on St. Johns Bluff would continue to serve its strategic importance. General James Oglethorpe, the English royal governor of Georgia, encamped nearby on his ill-fated campaign in taking St. Augustine in 1740. During the War Between the States, Confederate forces constructed a series of earthen fortifications upon the bluff. These earthworks protected the river from intrusions by Union gunboats. A Confederate battery can still be seen today adjacent to the reconstructed Ribault monument. Another fortification was built upon the bluff during the Spanish-American War.

The original site of Fort Caroline was washed away after the deepening of the river in the 1880s. During the 1950s the area was set aside for the National Park Service to establish a historic settlement to commemorate the landing of Ribault and Laudonniere. However, an NPS report on the reconstructed French fort recorded by the "Interpretive Prospectus" stated that

> reconstruction was based on the best information available at the time. Modifications were made because of the location. Specific inadequacies known are: Reproduction is on smaller scale; bricks are used in wall construction; concrete is used to stabilize entrance path; supports for palisades are historically incorrect; entrance was relocated to provide easier access; landscaping; relocation of flagpole; and angle of fort were changed to accommodate the present shoreline.

The report further stated that the replica of the French fort was situated about two to three hundred yards from the original fort site. The purpose of the park is to educate visitors of the first European conflict in the New World and of life during the sixteenth century. The park's next objective is to provide interpretation to the nearby Civil War earthworks and the Spanish-American War concrete battery as secondary themes. Therefore, the park is unique in the sense that it interprets more than four hundred years of fortifications in the St. Johns Bluff area.

FORT CAROLINE

Erected 1564

Fort Caroline, 1564.

Aerial view of Fort Caroline, Jacksonville. *Courtesy of National Park Service.*

Interior view of Fort Caroline.

Fort George

During the Seven Years' War (1756–63), France and Spain battled the British. The British captured Cuba and at the end of the war Spain ceded La Florida to the British to regain Cuba. The British arrived to occupy Pensacola in August 1763. They found the town and military stockade in poor condition. In 1765, engineers completed a new plat for Pensacola. Plans included enlarging the deteriorated stockade at the waterfront, the development of city streets and residential lots. By 1781 the city had over two hundred and fifty new dwellings.

To better defend the city, three new fortifications were built north of the waterfront stockade. Fort George was the first built by British forces under the command of General John Campbell in 1772. It became one of the major defenses of Pensacola, the capital of British West Florida. Several hundred yards north, on higher ground, the Queen's Redoubt and the Prince of Wales Redoubt were part of the system. Fort George consisted of a square parade ground, an earthen rampart with four demi-bastions, surrounded by a dry moat. The fort wall mounted twenty cannons. An outer earthwork stretched southwest for approximately six hundred feet.

King Carlos III of Spain appointed thirty-two-year-old Bernardo de Galvez governor general of Louisiana on January 1, 1777. He had proven skills as a soldier and military leader in campaigns at Portugal and New Spain. In 1779, Galvez captured British outposts on the Mississippi, then Mobile in 1780. In February 1781, Field Marshal Galvez led a convoy of thirty-two ships and three thousand men to seize British West Florida. During the sixty-one-day battle of Pensacola, Galvez was wounded by musket fire while leading his troops. The battle of Pensacola would be considered the greatest victory of his career.

Spanish forces consisted of some of the country's most elite regiments, including the Hibernian Infantry. Joining the Spanish force were grenadiers, dragoons and rangers of the Louisiana Regiment, a company of well-trained Irish soldiers, American volunteers and some eight hundred French rangers. Soldiers from Louisiana included free mulatto and Negro troops. Slaves served both the Spanish and British military. British forces included the elite British Sixtieth and Sixteenth Regiments of Foot, Pennsylvania, Maryland Loyalists and the Third Waldeck Regiment of German Mercenaries.

Entering Pensacola Bay, the Spanish prepared trenches and batteries from which to attack the British forces. The British requested that the town not be attacked and women, children and infirm be allowed sanctuary in the waterfront stockade. The battle centered on Fort George. In spite of being outnumbered three to one, the British held their position for two months. With reinforcements, Galvez commanded over seven thousand troops. Fort George was besieged for two weeks, April 24 to May 8, 1781. A Spanish shell from a howitzer penetrated the magazine of the Queen's Redoubt and exploded, killing and maiming much of the British garrison on the morning of May 8, 1781. The defenders raised the white flag at three in the afternoon and the following day the Spanish took in

A mini-park with a restored portion of Fort George's earthworks was established in 1976.

1,113 prisoners after the formal surrender; 105 of the British defenders were killed in the magazine blast.

The Spaniards began reconstruction of Fort George in 1783 and renamed it Fort San Miguel. The Queen's Redoubt was also renamed to Fort Bernando and the Prince of Wales Redoubt became Fort Sombrero. Only San Bernando was occupied. Consideration was given to abandoning the city in favor of an earlier site near the entrance to the bay. New fortifications were built at the harbor entrance. It was hoped that Pensacola's meager defenses could withstand a siege by Indian or European armies long enough for assistance to arrive from Havana.

Although Pensacola officially belonged to Spain after 1783, the British often used East Florida to harass the United States. In 1814, General Andrew Jackson invaded Florida to attack British forces. By the time of General Jackson's entrance into Pensacola, the earthen fortifications were in complete disrepair after bombardment by the Americans. Again in 1818, Jackson entered Pensacola, this time to stop Florida Indians from raiding the United States. In 1818, Jackson ordered the Spanish garrison be shipped to Havana and U.S. troops commanded by Colonel William King occupied the city and its forts for ten months. Jackson entered the city a third time in July 1821 to accept Florida from the last Spanish governor.

During the War Between the States, Fort McClellan, a Union-built defense on Palafox Hill where old Fort George stood, was erected in late 1862 and used by Federal forces during most of 1863. Interestingly, a Confederate war memorial is within the vicinity of the former Union fortification. During the nation's bicentennial a number of archeologists made a nine-month investigation of the site and their excavations revealed significant remains of both the British and Spanish forts. Several elements of the fort were located, including a section of the moat, a powder magazine and a group of vaulted rooms believed to be latrines. Since the site did not include living and dining areas, few artifacts were recovered. Much of the usable equipment was removed from the structure when it was abandoned. The findings helped recreate a portion of the defensive positions of Fort George and an area now preserved as a mini-park on the corner of Palafox and Jackson Streets.

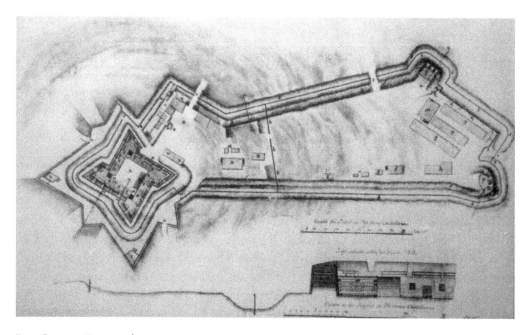

Fort George, Pensacola.

Spanish troops stormed the breached defenses of Fort George, 1781. *Courtesy of U.S. Army.*

Fort Matanzas

The history of Fort Matanzas and Matanzas Inlet began with the slaughter of Jean Ribault and his French Huguenot comrades by Pedro Menendez de Aviles in 1565. The area and waterway near the bloodied sands would bear the name Matanzas (or "slaughter") in memory of the events that occurred there. By 1569, a small wooden watchtower was established in order to protect the waterway that led to the backdoor of St. Augustine. Serious attention was given to Matanzas Inlet during the siege of St. Augustine in 1740.

English expansion into Spanish territory began with General James Oglethorpe's establishment of Savannah in 1733, marking the beginning of the colony of Georgia. In 1736, the English went farther south along Georgia's coast and established Fort Frederica near modern-day Brunswick. The Spanish denunciation of these encroachments fell upon deaf ears. With fear of further English expansion, the Spanish hierarchy began examining the fortifications and military strength in East Florida. Around November of 1736, Captain Antonio De Arredondo y Perez, a top military engineer who was sent by the Royal governor of Cuba to examine the condition of the Spanish defenses in East Florida, had stated in his report that the very southern end of Anastasia Island, where "the bar of Matanzas is situated…there is a guard stationed but without any shelter whatsoever." "This is abandoned to the insult of any class of enemies," reports the Fort Matanzas Stabilization Team.

During April of 1738, Arredondo returned to Florida with a fellow officer, Pedro Ruiz de Olano. The latter officer was appointed to be the resident engineer in Florida and was ordered to build new defenses around St. Augustine. The projects that would receive major priorities were the modernization of the Castillo de San Marcos and the construction of a new fort in de San Francisco de Pupo. Because of these major projects, the defenses of Matanzas Inlet were given low priority.

In an attempt to conquer Spanish-held Florida, General Oglethorpe decided to lay siege upon St. Augustine on June 13, 1740. Oglethorpe disguised his reason for annexing Florida by using the War of Jenkins's Ear as an excuse for the siege of the old Spanish town. The inlet and waterway of Matanzas were blockaded by several armed English warships. Their purpose was to prevent any supplies and re-enforcements from reaching the besieged city. Before the English blockade was completed, the Spanish governor Manuel de Montiano managed to send a courier to Cuba asking for provisions. The town had only enough supplies to feed its garrison and civilians for approximately three weeks.

In the early days of July, the blockading ships at Matanzas Inlet received orders to rejoin the other English warships at St. Augustine Inlet. This move permitted the Spanish ships from Cuba to enter the inlet and bring much-needed supplies to the Spanish defenders at St. Augustine. "Fearing the approach of the hurricane season, the British fleet decided to sail for safer waters. Lacking naval support and knowing that the city was now well supplied, Oglethorpe raised the siege on July 20, 1740," writes Haas in *Citadels, Ramparts and Stockades*. Serious considerations were then taken in fortifying the vulnerable approaches to St. Augustine, including the inlet and waterway of Matanzas.

Fearing another British invasion into Florida, Governor Montiano ordered the erection of a permanent fort on Matanzas Inlet without royal approval from Spain. Construction of the fort is believed to have begun in the fall or early winter of 1740, under the supervision of engineer Pedro Ruiz de Olano. The English were informed of the fort's construction by their Indian allies and several unsuccessful attempts were made to destroy the strategic Spanish fort. The new fort was located upon a small marshy island that was surrounded by the waters of the Matanzas River.

Building the fort was difficult, in that "long piles had to be driven deep into the mud to support the rising stonework," writes Haas. The fort's features were to include a gun deck that rose about eleven feet above the ground, a southeastern front that "had a low parapet, without embrasures or merlons. The low parapet furnished little or no protection to either the gun or the crew, but this was compensated by simpler construction, easier service of the piece, and wider field of fire. The east parapet was a breast-high wall with two embrasures," notes the Fort Matanzas Stabilization Team.

The fort's major design feature was its tower. The design was similar to the Martello Towers found all over Europe (in Key West, there are two modern Martello Towers that were built during the War Between the States and are similar to the one in Matanzas Inlet in shape and purpose). The tower section of the fort was to contain a cistern, a magazine and quarters for the commanding officer and his men. The capacity of the fort was for fifty men and six cannons. However, only four six-pounder and one eighteen-pounder cannons were ever stationed at the fort at one time. Fort Matanzas was finally completed sometime around 1742 and experienced its first battle soon after.

A second British attack on St. Augustine was attempted once more in September 1742. After being repulsed by the Spanish warships and batteries around St. Augustine Inlet, the British tried to enter St. Augustine's backdoor, Matanzas Inlet. The British believed that the fort was still under construction and that no retaliation would be given by the construction crew at the site. On September 10, 1742, two English ships sailed into the inlet to take soundings of the area. It was believed that General Oglethorpe was on one of these ships. "Reaching a point 3 ½ fathoms deep, within range of the 'unfinished fort,' the boats suddenly found themselves warned by a cannon shot fired from the now completed Fort Matanzas. One of the boats turned back immediately and the other did the same a very short time later," reports the Fort Matanzas Stabilization Team. The British force was later forced to return to their bases in Georgia, due to bad weather conditions and the now completed fort at Matanzas Inlet.

During the first few decades, Fort Matanzas never held its specified number of fifty men at any one time. Usually, the detachment stationed at the fort consisted of an officer, four infantry privates and two gunners. At times, during war, the small fort's garrison would rise up to ten men. If the fort was seriously threatened, then more additional men were sent in from St. Augustine. With Spain's declaration of war against England in 1762, the garrison at Fort Matanzas had reached up to ten men, which was not enough for effectively using all five cannons at the small outpost.

Spain's war with England resulted in the loss of the Spanish colony of Cuba. In return for Cuba, Spain promised to cede Florida to the British. A treaty was signed in Paris on February 10, 1763, and with that Florida became British. In an inspection report of Fort Matanzas, a British officer noted that "Matanzas is a tower, where the Spaniards had five guns which they have taken away, the garrison sends ten men hither, it serves to guard the lower bar at the south of the Island," writes the Fort Matanzas Stabilization Team. To prevent an Indian attack upon the small defenseless fort, a British officer recommended the installment of two six-pounder cannons. However, a ship carrying these much-needed cannons was sunk off the vicinity of St. Augustine. It wasn't until June of 1764 that the fort was finally armed with the two guns.

The garrison at Fort Matanzas fluctuated at times during the period of English occupation. In 1764, the small fort was garrisoned by a sergeant and eight privates. At other times the fort was garrisoned by a corporal and four or five privates. Of course, during times of war the small outpost's garrison would be increased; such was the case during the American Revolution. Detachments from the British Ninth Infantry Regiment were stationed at Fort Matanzas during most of the period of occupation.

The outbreak of the American Revolution had brought St. Augustine and Florida new importance, for the new English territory became a haven for British Loyalists fleeing persecution by colonists who had rebelled against English rule. The entire territory of Florida became an armed camp in which old defenses were rebuilt and new ones were built. The fort at Matanzas was found to be in good repair and no new modifications were added to the fort. Several attempts in seizing East Florida by American Rebels from Georgia were repulsed by the British garrison in St. Augustine. Plans for another Rebel invasion of Florida were destroyed when the British captured the Rebel-held seaport town of Savannah, Georgia, during November of 1778. The capture ended any Rebel influence in southern Georgia and East Florida during the remainder of the Revolution.

British officials in Florida feared the entry of Spain into the Revolutionary War, fighting on behalf of the American rebels. Again, forts in the Florida territory were to be prepared for any surprise attacks with Spain's declaration of war on June 21, 1779. By the fall of 1780, Fort Matanzas's garrison had risen to eleven men, consisting of a sergeant, a gunner and nine infantrymen. The fall of British-held Pensacola and East Florida to Bernardo de Galvez's Spanish forces in May of 1781 made British officials in St. Augustine fear a Spanish invasion of East Florida. Further plans were made to upgrade the outpost at Matanzas Inlet.

The British commander at St. Augustine, Brigadier General Archibald McArthur, ordered the reinforcement of the entrance to St. Augustine's backdoor, Fort Matanzas. The general "established the fort as headquarters for an officers' party and provided the fort with two eighteen-pounders. Brigadier General McArthur then upgraded the garrison at Matanzas by stationing a captain and thirty men at the fort. Also, a large and small galley were to be stationed in the harbor to support the troops," reported the Fort Matanzas Stabilization Team. It has been thought that during this period the southeastern parapet walls were strengthened with wood and earth construction and that the other embrasures of the fort were covered.

The American victory in Yorktown, Virginia, had ended any British hopes of retaining the North American colonies. Next to a peace treaty with the new United States of America, another British treaty was signed with Spain on September 3, 1783. The Anglo-Hispanic treaty gave Spain the remaining eastern part of Florida. Spanish possession of East Florida was taken when the new Spanish governor, Vicente Manuel de Cesepedes, and his troops marched into the gates of St. Augustine on July 12, 1784. On that date, the former British governor, Patrick Tonyn, and General McArthur surrendered St. Augustine and all fortifications to the new Spanish governor. During the first few years of the second Spanish rule in Florida, major concerns included the upgrading of defenses and of governmental buildings in St. Augustine. Therefore, maintenance of Fort Matanzas remained ignored for close to five years after the resumption of Spanish rule.

An inspection tour of Fort Matanzas was conducted by the head engineer, Mariano de la Rocque, from Castillo de San Marcos in 1789. Chatelain's *The Defenses of Spanish Florida, 1565 to 1763* provides the Spanish engineer's description of the small outpost in the following manner:

> *Opposite the mouth* [of the inlet] *about a distance of a short cannon shot, there is an islet where the castle is built, and it continues toward the interior* [i.e., the back country] *with a short half mile of marsh and mangrove. Walls of the said castle are of masonry, and there are inside quarters for the troops. Its sides are about twenty yards, and the parapet is made of wood filled with earth, with three embrasures opposite the bar, and three more on the north and south sides; consequently* [there is] *a capacity of nine guns…This place in peace time does not need another thing than maintaining the said castle in the state that now obtains.*

The wooden earth-filled parapet that was mentioned by de la Rocque was probably the one built by the English a few years before. The two six-pounder guns that were at the fort in 1783 were removed by the British when they evacuated East Florida.

Under the supervision of Commanding Engineer Mariano de la Rocque, repairs and maintenance for Fort Matanzas began sometime around 1789. By 1793, Spain had improved the gun deck at Fort Matanzas and two eight-pounder cannons were mounted on a barbette. The following year, the roof and cistern were repaired and cleaned for healthier use by the fort's small garrison. No records have been found on any further repairs or modifications on Fort Matanzas from 1784 to 1795. During the remaining few years of Spanish rule, the Spanish engineers had major problems in fixing the erosion of the foundation of the fort. Cracks formed throughout the fort's walls and water leakage in the magazine was reported in 1799. The fort's new role, next to protecting the waterway, was to guard against the stealing of coquina stones and oyster shells from a nearby government-owned quarry.

In 1809, extensive work was done on the fort when the second-story floor collapsed, damaging the chimney. The fort began to decay due to inconsistent repairs and maintenance upon the fort. By 1818, "the fort commander complained that the structure was in dire need of repairs, at a time when the resident engineer's position had been filled, after a five year and five month lapse, by Captain Francisco Cortazar. Cortazar inspected Fort Matanzas. He found that river erosion had exposed and destroyed part of the footing and undermined the scarp wall," reported the Fort Matanzas Stabilization Team. The fort's quarters were hardly a place to stay dry during rainy weather, due to cracks that had formed in the roof.

Due to the deteriorated condition of the fort, the fort's small garrison was forced to live in tents until repairs were made. When lightning struck the fort's roof around September of 1820, the structure became totally uninhabitable and useless for its purpose. Despite the conditions existing at the outpost, it was not abandoned. The soldiers continued living in tents or other temporary structures. The few guns were still maintained by the greatly reduced garrison and minimal care was given to the still-strategic outpost. Before the transfer of Florida to the United States, the fort's muster had listed only the following three soldiers: Sergeant Second Class Lorenzo Brito of the Colored Militia Company of Havana; Sergeant Second Class Manuel Ruiz of the Sixth Company, Second Battalion, Infantry Regiment of Cuba; and Gunner Francisco de Herrera of the Corps of National Artillery.

On July 10, 1821, both East and West Florida were ceded by Spain to the United States. Ownership and maintenance of all former Spanish defenses, including Fort Matanzas, were acquired by the War Department. The outpost's strategic importance was lost when Florida became part of the United States and there was no need to protect it from enemies who no longer had nearby bases from which to wage their attacks. Soon the structure was overrun with vegetation and the sentry box, the south parapet's central merlon, the stairway, the various doors and windows, the roof and the chimney were all missing. It wasn't until the 1880s, nearly forty years later, that the War Department began to take an interest in Fort Matanzas.

The fort was discovered by northern tourists and Florida travel books began mentioning the site in the early 1880s. One of these books, *The Standard Guide for St. Augustine*, mentions that the old Spanish "ruins are among the most picturesque in Florida. In the early morning and at sunset the fort and its surroundings present a scene

Fort Matanzas as it appeared at the turn of the nineteenth century.

of beauty well worth the journey to behold," reports the Fort Matanzas Stabilization Team. Due to the interest of frequent visitors, the War Department began to treat the site as an interesting relic from the days of Spanish colonialism. A team of army engineers surveyed the fort and surrounding area in 1885. The engineers believed that the fort no longer had any military importance; but they recommended that the fort be preserved for its historical importance.

It wasn't until 1915 and 1916 that Congress allotted some money for the preservation of Fort Matanzas and designated the fort a national landmark. For the next eighteen years or so the site underwent major reconstruction under the supervision of the Army Corps of Engineers and later by the Quartermaster Corps. The fort's status was upgraded to national monument in 1924. On July 10, 1933, the War Department ceded Fort Matanzas to the Department of the Interior and instructed that the site was to be maintained by the National Park Service. Since the acquisition of the fort, careful historical research on the fort's structure has been carried out for ongoing renovation. Today, the park contains a visitor's center and ferry service to Fort Matanzas.

Fort Matanzas as it appears today. *Courtesy of National Park Service.*

FORT MOSE

The fort and the community of Gracia Real de Santa Teresa de Mose, located two miles north of St. Augustine, were established in 1738 by escaped slaves from the English colony of Carolina who were granted their freedom in Spanish St. Augustine. The men were made members of the Spanish militia and the fort served as Florida's first line of defense against the English to the north. The garrison was led by Francisco Menendez, captain of the Fort Mose black militia, and arrived in St. Augustine from Carolina around 1724. The majority of the members of the black militia were born free in West Africa, where they were captured and transported across the Atlantic Ocean. Enslaved in America, they risked their lives to escape captivity by traveling a rough and dangerous path through frontier Georgia.

Fort Mose had log walls reinforced with an earthen berm. It enclosed thatched huts and was ringed with a ditch containing "prickly palmetto royal" or "Spanish Bayonets." Surrounding it were farm fields, homes for the freedmen and salt marsh. During the siege of St. Augustine by General James Oglethorpe, the garrison was forced to abandon Fort Mose in order to reinforce St. Augustine's garrison in May 1740. Troops under the command of Captain Hugh Mackay and Colonel John Palmer occupied the fort in June. On June 26, 1740, a British soldier recounted the following events that took place at "Bloody Mose":

At one in the morning some of the Rangers reported that they had heard the Spanish Indians dancing the War Dance. At Four o'Clock the Colonel went to rouse them, to stand to their Arms. But as usual, most of them lay down again. This put him into great Passion, saying that the Spaniards would surely attack them after the Indian Manner and that General Oglethorpe had sent them there for a sacrifice. Then a Centinel called that a Party was coming and Colonel Palmer called aloud, "Stand to your arms! Not a Man of you fire, but receive their first fire; then half of you fire and fall back, making Room for the rest to come up, and we will kill them like Dogs."

Then poured in a large Volley, and the Colonel betook himself to the ditch. The Rangers did the same. [The Indians' leader] run into the Fort, and got all the Indians together into one Flanker, there being a great Hurry and Confusion, some being dressed and some undressed. The Enemy attacking in different Parties, rushed on...Colonel Palmer in the Trench, kept firing and encouraging the Men aloud, and the Spaniards were repulsed twice. At length they came on again Sword in Hand and entered the Gate. At the same Time another Party entered one of the breaches, so that the Fort was at once full of Spaniards, it being then about Half an Hour before Day. Firing as they marched and opening a Passage for themselves through the Enemy, [thirty-five British] made their escape. The Spaniards, as it pleased God, did nor pursue their Victory; but marched back to their Castle in great Triumph, shouting and firing in Sight of the Camps with the Prisoners and Colours that they had taken in the Fort.

In conclusion, Don Manuel de Montiano, Spanish governor of La Florida, wrote:

At 11 o'clock on the night of Saturday, 25 June, I sent out from this garrison three hundred men to make an attack on the Fort of Mose, which was executed at day-break on Sunday morning. Our people swept over it, with such impetuosity that it fell with a loss of sixty-eight dead and thirty-four prisoners. An Indian prisoner affirms positively that he saw Colonel Palmer dead and his head cut off...The affair being terminated, I ordered the fort to be demolished, and the dead buried.

Eventually Oglethorpe's siege failed and the British retreated back to Georgia. In 1742, Montiano invaded Georgia in retaliation but was defeated at the battle of Bloody Marsh near Fort Frederica on Saint Simon's Island.

Only a few hundred feet from the first site of the ruined defenses, Fort Mose and its surrounding community were rebuilt in 1752. When Spain ceded Florida to the British in 1763, the second site of Fort Mose had been described as a sizeable village of thatched huts with a chapel and a fort with a lookout tower and two cannon-mounted bastions, surrounded by a moat. In 1775 the British dismantled Fort Mose. Today both sites that made up the fort are preserved by the Florida Park Service within the Fort Mose Historic State Park.

Fort St. Marks

The site of Fort San Marcos de Apalache vividly tells of Florida's varied and colorful past; a past that ranges from the Spaniards who built the fort to the Confederates who rebuilt and defended this little strategic outpost in the confluence of the Wakulla and the St. Marks Rivers. The first fort was built sometime between 1679 and 1680, during the first Spanish period (from 1679, when construction of the fort began, to 1763, when Spanish troops relinquished control of the fort to British occupational troops). The rough logs used in the construction of the fort were coated with lime in order to give the appearance of stone.

On March 20, 1682, a pirate ship moved silently up the river to the unfinished Fort San Marcos de Apalache. Sighting a merchant ship anchored there, the pirate launched three pirogues for an attack against the Spanish installation. One pirogue crew boarded and captured the merchant ship, while the other two attacked the fort. During the engagement, the pirates set fire to and eventually captured the fort, taking the Spaniards prisoner. The Spaniards immediately rebuilt the outpost, only to have it attacked again on June 8. A second pirate attack and frequent English incursions into Florida forced the Spaniards to destroy the fort and leave the area for a while. These English incursions occurred sometime between 1700 and 1706.

Those short years were known as the War of Succession (Queen Anne's War). In 1704, the English governor of South Carolina, James Moore, attacked "the missions and smaller garrisons of Apalache. Around August of 1706 the English and their savage allies, the Creeks, have leveled all the area north of Florida, from the Apalachicola to the St. Johns," writes Marban in *Florida: Five Centuries of Hispanic History*. The surviving Spanish soldiers in the area fled to either Pensacola or St. Augustine. "During the period of abandonment this wooden fort of San Marcos must have fallen into complete decay," reports Boyd in "The Fortifications at San Marcos de Apalache."

In 1718, the French were found to be exploring St. Joseph's Bay and erecting stockade huts and trading stations there. The Spanish ordered the French to leave the bay area and made preparations to remove them forcibly if it became necessary. The French were not prepared to fight and retreated. In March of that same year Captain Jose Primo de Ribera was sent to rebuild and modify the old wooden fort for a full-time garrison to man the strategic outpost.

The next year, as a reflection of the war in Europe, the French surprised and took the Spanish fortress at Pensacola. It changed hands several times before the French finally burned the fort and the settlement. They sailed away when the Spanish abandoned St. Joseph's Bay, leaving Fort St. Marks as the sole military installation west of the Aucilla River for more than a year.

The construction of the stone fort, the foundation of which still exists today, began in 1739. Due to the inaccessibility of the location the fort construction was slow. When formal occupation of the fort was handed down to the British in 1763, the outpost was not even half-finished (nearly twenty-four years after construction had begun in 1739). "In fact it would appear that as late as 1758 it was so incomplete that the garrison was housed in the old wooden fort. A hurricane that year flooded the old fort, drowning forty men," writes Boyd in "The Fortifications at San Marcos de Apalache."

As a result of the French and Indian War, a war in which Spain was wheedled by the French into hostilities with Britain on January 1762 and a war that took Florida from Spain for the next twenty years, English troops occupied Fort San Marcos de Apalache. The British occupation of the fort was from 1763 to 1769. Due to the scarcity of food and supplies, the English soldiers returned to St. Augustine to wait out the occupation after only six years at St. Marks. It wasn't until 1787 that Spanish troops would reoccupy the fort. The second Spanish period was quiet for the next thirteen years. However, four hundred Indians, under the command of ex-English officer William Augustus Bowles, captured Fort San Marcos. Bowles, who proclaimed himself to be the king of Florida, was ousted from control of the fort by Spanish troops five weeks later.

Due to Spain's inability to control the Indians and to prevent them from making raids from Florida, President Monroe gave Andrew Jackson, a general in the U.S. Army, the task of solving the Indian problem in the South. The Southern frontier had long been disrupted by skirmishes between the rival powers. As a last attempt to secure their dwindling position in the new world, England and Spain encouraged the Indians, who needed little provocation, to annoy the American pioneers expanding their frontiers into Indian territory.

To ensure the safety and interests of the Americans in the area, Jackson found it necessary to quell the Indians by force. The intervention into Spanish Florida marked the First Seminole War of 1817–18. Declaring martial law, General Jackson commandeered the Spanish-held Fort San Marcos and made it his Indian-fighting headquarters. The fort's strategic location made it an ideal place for punishing prisoners of war, disobedient Indians and rebellious Europeans. An incident concerning Jackson's treatment of European prisoners led him and his country into a serious diplomatic crisis with Great Britain known as the Arbuthnot and Ambrister Incident of 1818.

The Arbuthnot-Ambrister Affair at Fort San Marcos caused more commotion than any other incident of the highly controversial First Seminole War. Arbuthnot had charge of the Forbes Company at Fort San Marcos. When Jackson commandeered the fort, Arbuthnot was taken prisoner and charged with spying and inciting the Indians. At his court-martial, Arbuthnot was found guilty and sentenced to be hanged.

Ambrister was captured by a party of Jackson's men returning from a futile attempt to capture Chief Bowlegs (Bolecks) village. They found in Ambrister's possession a letter from Arbuthnot warning Bowlegs of Jackson's plan to attack. Ambrister was also court-martialed, found guilty and sentenced to be shot. Both he and Arbuthnot were executed on the day Jackson left Fort San Marcos, April 29, 1818. With Jackson's withdrawal from the fort Spanish troops were able to re-occupy the installation. Jackson's troops left behind nineteen of their fellow comrades at St. Marks, who died of illnesses during their occupation of 1817–18. The British anger over the execution of two of its subjects was appeased with apologies from U.S. military officers and by a payment of indemnity to the bereaved families. Thus, a third war with Britain was avoided. The incident later came up to haunt the presidential election of General Andrew Jackson.

The end of Spanish dominance in the region came in 1821 when Florida was ceded to the United States. Plans were made for the transfer of power between Spanish and American troops in Fort St. Marks. As Young reports in "The Transfer of Fort San Marcos and East Florida to the United States," the ceremony began with a

> *salute fired by the fort on Tuesday morning, on hoist the Spanish flag. During the disembarcation of the American troops, the flag of the United States will be hoisted along with the Spanish flag, when the fort will again fire a salute. The American officer who delivers the flag to remain in the fort until its delivery. When the American troops are formed near the fort the Spanish flag will be withdrawn under a salute; the guards will then be relieved, and the troops of Spain will march out, and, on passing the former, they will mutually salute; when the American troops will be marched in to and occupy the fortress.*

On Tuesday, July 10, 1821, everything went according to the plan. Immediately after the transfer of power, U.S. troops occupied the fort for three years and in 1824 the fort was turned over to the territorial government of Florida. Fifteen years later, in 1839, the fort was returned to the U.S. government and a federal marine hospital was constructed near the site with materials from the crumbling old Spanish fort. The hospital was for the care of yellow fever victims and the structure was completed in 1858. The United States abandoned the hospital with the outbreak of the Civil War and the hospital building slowly disintegrated with time. Today the San Marcos de Apalache State Historic Site Museum stands on the foundations of this old hospital.

With the outbreak of the War Between the States in 1861, Confederate forces re-garrisoned the old fort and renamed it Fort Ward. The fort served as a deterrent to the Union naval forces and prevented penetration inland from the Gulf. No major battles were fought at the fort and life at St. Marks during the war continued much as it had previously. The fort would remain in Confederate hands until the end of the Civil War.

Earthen and wooden barricades were built over the ruins of the old Spanish fort. Protective earthworks were erected along the south wall of the bombproof. The Confederates also covered the north, west and east walls. A powder magazine was located on a large hill behind the foundations of the curtain wall. It was also surrounded by earthworks, which gave protected access to two gun emplacements. One emplacement was located on the remains of the Bastion of San Fernando to the west and the other on the remains of the bombproof. Both emplacements were enclosed by earthworks with a core of rubble taken from the Spanish fort and were braced with rows of wooden posts. Inside each emplacement was a large gun platform with a sloping floor of heavy wooden planks, which absorbed the recoil of the cannons.

A gap was made in the curtain wall foundation as an entrance for access from the powder magazine to the gun enclosure. An artillery company also manned a barricade on the east bank of the river near the lighthouse. The face of the old Spanish fort underwent major changes with the additions of these earthworks and the relocation of some of the fort's rubble. Union naval officers, who had established an effective blockade off the mouth of the St. Marks River, regarded the Confederate batteries at St. Marks with great respect.

In February 1864, two Union Naval expeditions destroyed the salt works at St. Marks and Goose Creek, together valued at $4 million and capable of producing 2,500 bushels of salt a day. But Fort Ward would face near-destruction when "on the afternoon of March 4, 1865, fourteen vessels landed approximately one thousand troops at the lighthouse near St. Marks, and began obvious preparation to move inland," writes Johns in *Florida During the Civil War*. The following day, on March 5, 1865, Union Army troops, under the command of General John Newton, advanced on Newport, thereby threatening Tallahassee.

The Federals' main plan was to capture Fort Ward and Port Leon, with the help of naval units under the leadership of Commander William Gibson. The Confederates, under command of Brigadier General William Miller, discovered the advance in time to summon reinforcements to stop the Union forces. The Confederate general, after learning that the officer in charge of Fort Ward was alerted of the near proximity of the Union fleet and "was preparing to blow up the magazine, burn the gun-boat *Spray*, and put fire to some 600 bales of cotton at the port, set off at once for St. Marks, fortunately arriving before these designs were consummated. His orders put an end to all thought of surrender at that place," reports Boyd in "Joint Operations of the Federal Army and Navy near St. Marks." After saving the fort from certain destruction, General Miller returned to his command in Newport and prepared to face the Federal force in the area of Natural Bridge.

Poor communications, bad weather and Confederate alertness defeated the Union army in the battle of Natural Bridge near Newport. When the Union Naval units were advised of the army's defeat, they abandoned further efforts to ascend the river. Union losses consisted of 21 killed, 89 wounded and 148 missing. However, Confederate losses consisted of 3 killed and 23 wounded. Tallahassee was the only Confederate state capital east of the Mississippi never captured by Union forces.

On May 12, 1865, Union forces received the fort's formal surrender from the Confederate defenders and "there Fort Ward was occupied and two small Confederate gunboats appropriated," writes Davis in *The Civil War and Reconstruction in Florida*. The surrender marked the end of the Civil War in Florida and the end of the military presence

Fort San Marcos de Apalache. *Courtesy of Florida Park Service.*

in Fort Ward (formerly Fort San Marcos de Apalache). For the next century the fort site slowly fell into disrepair and disintegration.

"In 1892 all of the area embraced in the military reservation was transferred to the general land office, and replatted in conformity with the original survey, including the fort itself. All lots in this area were sold, so that the ruin of Fort St. Marks" was in private hands, according to Boyd's "The Fortifications at San Marcos de Apalache." But, by act of Congress and by approval of President John F. Kennedy, Fort San Marcos de Apalache was designated a national historic landmark in 1962. On January 11, 1966, the site was made a state historic site with a museum to be established on the former foundations of the marine hospital. Today, this historic site is preserved for future generations to walk about within its old ramparts.

Spanish ruins of the fort with remains of the Confederate magazine of Fort Ward in the background.

The keystone to the arch of the bombproof of Fort San Marcos is preserved in the museum adjacent to the fort's ruins.

Fort San Carlos

The land above the Amelia River was a campsite for Indians in prehistoric times, as early as 2000–1000 BC. In the early history of the states, it assumed military importance because of the fine protected harbor on the northern boundary of Spanish Florida. In the first Spanish period, a village of Franciscans and Indians was established by 1675, and a Spanish sentinel's house was documented in 1696. From 1736 to 1742, James Oglethorpe, British governor of Georgia, stationed Highlanders on this site. After the withdrawal of Oglethorpe's troops in 1742, the area served as a buffer zone between the English and the Spanish until 1763 when Florida became a British possession. When Spain regained possession of Florida in 1783, the harbor became an embarkation point for British Loyalists leaving Florida. The U.S. Embargo Act of 1807, which closed all U.S. ports to European trade, made the border town of Fernandina a center for smuggling. The town of Fernandina was situated on a peninsula that was defended by a strong picket and two blockhouses that enclosed the whole town. On March 17, 1812, a group of Americans known as the Patriots overthrew the Spanish battery, but the U.S. flag replaced the Patriots' standard after one day. Spain regained control in May 1813 and completed Fort San Carlos, which protected the harbor side of Fernandina, in 1816.

The fort was made of wood and earthworks and was armed with eight or ten guns. As the fort's parade ground, the site was named Plaza San Carlos and was located on Estrada Street. As the Spanish empire disintegrated, Fort San Carlos became increasingly vulnerable to foreign intervention. Commissioned by representatives of revolting South American countries to liberate Florida from Spanish control, Sir Gregor MacGregor seized the fort in June 1817. After his withdrawal in September, the Spanish attempt to reassert their authority was repelled by forces led by MacGregor's lieutenants, Jared Irwin and Ruggle Hubbard.

On September 13 the battle of Amelia occurred when Spaniards erected a battery of four brass cannons on McClure's Hill. With about three hundred men, supported by two gunboats, they began shelling Fernandina, held by Jared Irwin, adventurer and former Pennsylvanian congressman. His "Republic of Florida" forces numbered ninety-four, the privateers *Morgiana* and *St. Joseph* and the armed schooner *Jupiter*. Spanish gunboats commenced firing at 3:30 p.m. and the battery on the hill joined the cannonade. Guns of Fort San Carlos, on the river bluff northwest of the hill, and those of the *St. Joseph* defended Amelia Island. Cannon balls killed two and wounded other Spanish troops concentrated below the hill. Firing continued until dark. The Spanish commander, convinced he could not capture the island, withdrew his forces.

Somewhat later, the pirate Luis Aury gained control of the fort. Because Aury's privateering threatened negotiations concerning the cession of Florida, United States troops occupied Fort San Carlos in December 1817. Although upset by U.S. interference at Fort San Carlos, Spain ceded Florida in 1821 and the U.S. abandoned the fort shortly after the transferal. Archeologists estimate that two-thirds of the fort disappeared through erosion. Along Estrada Street are traces of earthworks and the former parade ground of Fort San Carlos.

Only the parade ground and scant traces of the earthworks are left of Fort San Carlos on Amelia Island.

Spaniards established a battery on McClure's Hill and took part in the battle of Amelia on September 13, 1817.

Fort San Luís de Apalachee

As early as 1607, Apalachee chiefs asked the Spanish governor of La Florida to send friars to their province; Franciscan friars made a friendly visit the following year. In 1633 the friars established the mission of San Luís de Jinayca and by 1645 the first deputy governor of Apalachee was appointed. In 1647 non-Christian Indians staged an uprising in which seven of the eight existing churches were destroyed and the deputy governor, his family and three friars were murdered. Mission San Luís de Jinayca and a large native population moved to the present location, off present-day Mission Road and Ocala Road in Tallahassee, in 1656 and by this time the mission was recognized as the provincial capital. The Spaniards and native inhabitants built residential areas, an Apalachee Council House, Spanish fort and a Franciscan religious complex. The fort was an extensive, palisaded and fortified town in the form of an irregular parallelogram with bastions in its angles and a blockhouse, approximately ninety by sixty feet, in the center and the whole surrounded by a moat. The fort and

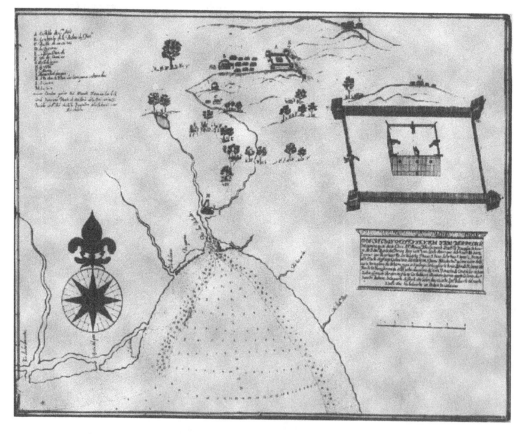

Fort San Luís from a survey made by Admiral Antonio de Landeche in 1705. *Courtesy of Florida State Archives.*

mission served as headquarters for seven missionary settlements in the Tallahassee area. By 1675, with a population of more than fifteen hundred people, San Luís was the largest community in the province. A new name, San Luís de Talimali, first appeared in Spanish documents.

War broke out between Britain and Spain in 1702 with forces of British Governor Oglethorpe threatening Spanish East Florida. An army of fifty Carolinians and approximately one thousand allied Creek Indians led by Colonel James Moore invaded East Florida in January 1704 and destroyed five of the Apalachee missions. After two more missions were destroyed in June, the Spanish evacuated Fort San Luís in July and blew up the fort and blockhouse. In recognition of its historical significance, San Luís was designated a national historic landmark in 1960 and was purchased by the State of Florida in 1983. In February 2006 reconstruction of the fort began on the site.

Fort San Luís was completely reconstructed on the original site in 2006–7.

Interior view of the living quarters within the blockhouse of Fort San Luís.

While outside the scope of this work, Fort Condé in Mobile, Alabama, was once part of West Florida during the Spanish period and played a part in Galvez's retaking of West Florida for Spain.

The Presidio Santa Maria de Galve, founded in 1696 by Spanish colonists, was in the area of Fort Barrancas at Naval Air Station Pensacola in northwest Florida. The presidio was captured peacefully on May 14, 1719, by Governor Bienville of French Louisiana, with a fleet of ships and a large ground force of Indian warriors. A hurricane devastated the area in 1722, and the evacuating French occupation forces burned the settlement before leaving. The Spanish forces rebuilt the region in 1722 as Fort San Carlos, in the area of Fort San Carlos de Barrancas. Seen here is the reconstructed northwest bastion of Presidio Santa Maria de Galve within the Pensacola Naval Air Station.

One of the cannons recovered from the site that has been stabilized and placed as part of the display of the reconstructed fortification of Santa Maria de Galve.

Above, left: The Pensacola Historical Society has numerous artifacts relating to the colonial period and relics from the forts built by the Spanish and British troops.

Above, right: Cannon shot and a fragment post from one of the British stockade fortifications in Pensacola.

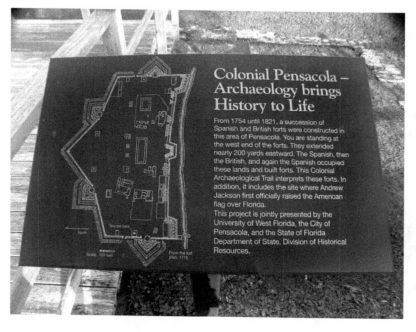

Throughout the oldest part of Pensacola, where Seville Square is located, are numerous markers pointing to sites where British fortifications and military buildings were located during the Spanish siege in 1781.

Above: Foundation of the officers' quarters within the British fortification near Seville Square, Pensacola.

Below: Remnants of the kitchens of the British commanding officers' compound located across the street from the Pensacola Historical Society's museum.

Chapter Two
THE TERRITORIAL ERA
AND THE SEMINOLE WARS

FORT BROOKE

The former Spanish colony of La Florida became a territory of the United States of America in 1821. After the rough campaigns of the First Seminole War, United States agents and representatives of the Seminoles signed the Camp Moultrie Treaty in 1823. This treaty specified a reservation for the Seminoles in the central part of Florida. A series of forts were to be built securing the boundaries of the reservation. Adding a military presence in the Tampa Bay area would provide a major source of protection from Seminoles desiring to break their treaty and possibly obtain weapons from smugglers coming out of Cuba. Colonel James Gadsden informed Secretary of War Calhoun that establishing a post in the Tampa Bay area was highly recommended because it "would demonstrate the military power of the white man and would serve as a means of keeping the Seminoles within the reservation," according to Covington's "Life at Fort Brooke." On November 5, 1823, Lieutenant-Colonel George Mercer Brooke received orders from the War Department to take four companies of the Fourth United States Infantry Regiment to Tampa Bay and establish a post.

The Fourth Infantry had been encamped in Cantonment Clinch since the early summer of 1823 (first post return dated July 1823). This post, located near Pensacola, had been the site of an encampment for Andrew Jackson's troops during his first campaign against the Seminoles in 1814 and again when Florida was transferred to the United States in 1821. The schooners *William*, *Henry* and *Rachael*, along with three transports, took Brooke's officers and men on their voyage on January 15, 1824, and arrived in Tampa Bay on January 18. A search party from the transports located a letter from Colonel Gadsden, who was surveying land for the new fort site, ordering Brooke to meet with him at his encampment at the juncture of the Hillsborough River and Hillsborough Bay. Upon their meeting, the two senior officers surveyed the area and decided upon building the post on the northeastern bank of the Hillsborough

River where the river emptied into Hillsborough Bay. Men began unloading their equipment, supplies and materiel from the transports and makeshift shelters began to appear in the Florida wilderness. The birth of Cantonment Brooke had begun.

At the outbreak of the Second Seminole War, "the whole military force then stationed in Florida, amounted to four hundred and eighty-nine men, including officers, and were distributed as follows: At St. Augustine, one company, fifty three men, including officers; at Fort Brooke on Hillsboro Bay, three companies, one hundred and thirty three men; at Fort King, six companies, three hundred and three men," writes Woodburne Potter in *The War in Florida*.

With the impending outbreak of hostilities with the Seminoles, Cantonment Brooke was changed to Fort Brooke in 1835. The change was in name only, for the installation resembled more of a frontier post with scattered buildings rather than a walled fortress. The post was actually a depot for in- and outgoing troops and supplies. The only fortified structures on the post were the prisoner's pen and Fraser's Redoubt (an earthwork and stockade that served as part of the ordnance department's complex of buildings). St. Augustine and Fort Brooke both served as a seat of command for U.S. troops interchangeably throughout the war.

The interwar years were a relatively peaceful decade for the fort, with its garrison being downsized to less than a thousand men at any one point in time. A severe hurricane destroyed most of the structures of Fort Brooke in 1847. The post was rebuilt with structures needed at the time, namely the officers' and enlisted men's barracks. The war with Mexico took three companies, leaving the fort with a twenty-two-man detachment from the Third U.S. Artillery Regiment. Later the post was reinforced with detachments from the First U.S. Artillery Regiment. Indian problems began to occur in 1849 and troops from Fort Brooke, mostly elements from the Seventh Infantry and Third Artillery, built three blockhouses and named them Fort Chokonikla (near present-day Bowling Green).

The Third Seminole War (1855–58) was fought mostly by Florida volunteer units. The fort was briefly reactivated and manned by elements of the Fifth and Seventh U.S. Infantry and Second and Fourth U.S. Artillery Regiments. After the war the fort fell under caretaker status and the post was transferred to the Department of the Interior. Soon portions of the reservation were leased to James McKay, a sea captain.

Upon the cessation of hostilities between the United States and the Confederate States, the post was seized by a local unit called the Tampa Guards under the command of John T. Lesley (who would later serve as captain with Company K, Sunny South Guards, Fourth Florida Volunteers). Numerous units were mustered into Confederate service at Fort Brooke: Twentieth Regiment of Florida Militia; Florida Volunteer Coast Guard; Company K, Fourth Florida; Company K, Seventh Florida; Company B, First Battalion, Florida Special Cavalry (also known as Captain John T. Lesley's Company, Independent Company of Mounted Volunteers of Munnerlyn's Battalion). For most of the war the post was garrisoned by the Osceola

Rangers, commanded by J.W. Pearson. A battery of three old naval twenty-four-pounder cannons were part of the fort's defenses (two of these cannons still exist, mounted on cement pedestals in Hyde Park, University of Tampa grounds).

Occasional Federal raids into the Tampa Bay area occurred throughout the Civil War. The fort came under various Union bombardments, beginning in April 1862, June 1862, July 1862, April 1863, October 1863 and December 1863. On May 6, 1864, a small Union force consisting of elements from the Second U.S. Colored Infantry seized Fort Brooke and Tampa with no opposition. The occupation was short-lived and the area was abandoned on May 12. No further major military activities occurred at the fort throughout the duration of the war.

PEACE AND THE END OF AN ERA, 1865–1882

During the years of Reconstruction, various Federal troops were stationed in Fort Brooke from time to time. Post returns were dated May 1865, July 1865 and April 1866. Elements of the Fifth U.S. Artillery Regiment were stationed at the fort from 1866 to 1869. These years of Union occupation were relatively quiet. From 1870 to 1874, the fort was again transferred to the Department of the Interior and an army quartermaster sergeant supervised the care of the site. A report stated that the reservation consisted of five frame buildings (including two long barracks), the collector's building and two houses. From May to October 1876, Companies G and H of the Fifth U.S. Artillery Regiment reoccupied the fort. The companies again returned in June 1877 and remained there until October 1877. The troops were from the Key West Barracks and spent their summer months in Tampa, where the climate was healthy by their standards. In May 1880 Companies D and E of the Fifth U.S. Artillery Regiment re-garrisoned Fort Brooke and remained there until January 1883. The military reservation ceased to exist after January 4, 1883.

Prior to the garrison's withdrawal a visitor noted in "Letters to Harriet Tracy Axtell," "We walked all over the old parade ground and I send Mama some blossoms picked from a Pinack bush on the old mound. The shore where our house are the earth works thrown up by the Confederate soldiers when Tampa was shelled…The row of mulberry trees that stood in front of Capt. Scriven's has grown to be gigantic, and all beyond is a thick growth of young trees and shrubs…Our' old oak tree is still there, grey with moss. The old buildings are gone, and the soldiers living in tents. Of course the gravel walks are all obliterated, but the trees looked very natural—even the old lime trees." The numerous historical markers that signified various sites of the Fort Brooke Military Reservation have gradually disappeared over the decades. The only trace that the fort ever existed are the two spiked naval guns from the Confederate battery mounted on the grounds of the University of Tampa.

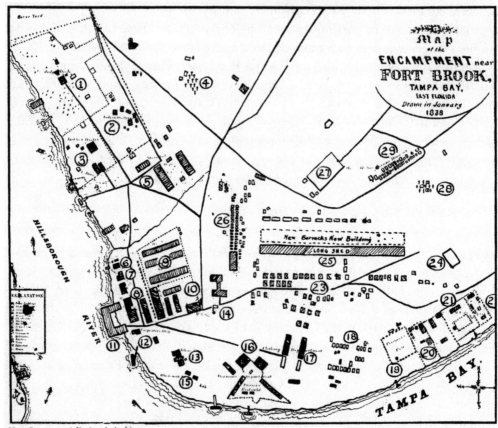

Map Courtesy of National Archives

Fort Brooke was one of the largest military establishments in the United States when this map was made in January, 1838. Legend: 1—Judge Augustus Steele's home and out-buildings. 2—Indian dwellings. 3—James Lynch's home and store. 4—United States cemetery. 5—Hospital buildings. 6—Sutler's store. 7—Bakehouse. 8—Commissary buildings. 9—Horse sheds. 10—Quartermaster buildings. 11—Principal wharf. 12—Carpenter's shop. 13—Allen's store. 14—Flag pole. 15—Blacksmith shop. 16—Ordnance department buildings and Major Frazer's redoubt. 17—Clothing department. 18—Uncovered marquees. 19—Prisoners' pen. 20—Major Fraser's quarters. 21—Lieut. McCrab's quarters. 22—Capt. Evan's quarters. 23—Covered marquees. 24—Horse shelter. 25—Barracks. 26—Uncovered marquees. 27—Horse shelter. 28—Cemetery. 29—German Dragoons.

Fort Brooke, 1838. *Courtesy of National Archives.*

Fort Brooke as it appeared in an 1846 illustration. Courtesy of Tampa-Hillsborough County Public Library System.

In the years following the Civil War, Fort Brooke served as a summer home for men of the Fifth U.S. Artillery Regiment from the Key West Barracks. *Courtesy of Tampa-Hillsborough County Public Library System.*

THE OLD BARRACKS, OLD FORT BROOKS, TAMPA, FLA.

Officers' quarters at Fort Brooke as it appeared at the turn of the nineteenth century.

OFFICERS QUARTERS
FORT BROOKE

MAJ. GEN. ANDREW JACKSON
(1st Provisional Governor of Florida)
(7th President of the United States)

First Recommended This Area As A
Military Site In 1818
(established 1824)
During the 1st Seminole Indian War

BRIG. GEN. ZACHARY TAYLOR
(12th President of the United States)

Commanded From Here, 1838-1840.
the U.S. Army
in 2nd Seminole Indian War.

One of the few remaining historical markers commemorating the location of the officers' quarters of Fort Brooke on Brorien Street. Over the years other historical markers related to Fort Brooke have disappeared due to vandalism and constant redevelopment in downtown Tampa.

The last remaining visible relics of Fort Brooke are two of the three naval guns that formed part of the Confederate battery during the Civil War. A historical marker describing the history of the guns disappeared years ago. The third gun was said to have been scrapped during World War II as a patriotic gesture.

Fort Christmas

On December 17, 1837, a column under the command of Brigadier General Abrahm Eustis left Fort Mellon (present-day Sanford) for campaign against the Seminoles farther south and to build additional military roads through the Florida wilderness. The column consisted of elements from the Third Regiment Artillery, four companies of the Third and Fourth Dragoons and four companies of Alabama volunteers. A supply depot was established on the north side of Christmas Creek and the post was named Fort Christmas, since construction began on that day. The fort was built eighty feet square of pine pickets with two substantial blockhouses twenty feet square. Supplies were brought in from Fort Lane and the dragoons were sent out on Christmas Day to establish Fort McNeil.

Between Forts Mellon and Christmas, the column constructed upward of twenty bridges varying in length from twenty to seventy feet. Major General Thomas S. Jessup, overall commander in Florida, led the column south from Fort Christmas early in January 1838, leaving Major Lomax and two companies of the Third Artillery to serve as the fort's garrison. By the end of the month Jessup's troops were receiving supplies by water through Jupiter Inlet and Fort Christmas was abandoned. The fort site lent its name to a community that sprung up in the years following the Second Seminole War. The Orange County Board of Commissioners and the Orange County Parks Department began reconstruction of Fort Christmas approximately half a mile from the original site on December 17, 1975. The fort was completed on December 17, 1977, and is one of the few sites with a museum, located within one of the blockhouses, devoted to the history of the Second Seminole War.

Fort Christmas near Orlando.

The interior of Fort Christmas.

A museum devoted to the history of the Second Seminole War (1835–42) can be found in one of the blockhouses.

Fort Cooper was a hastily constructed stockade that withstood a two-week siege by the Seminoles in April 1836. Today it is a state park located near Inverness.

Fort Dallas

The army established Fort Dallas in late January or early February 1838 on a high bluff near the mouth of the Miami River, on the inner shore of Biscayne Bay in present-day Dade County. There are two theories as to how the fort received its name. One possibility is that the fort was named after Commodore Alexander James Dallas, naval commander of the Caribbean Fleet, as requested by General Winfield Scott. But a microfilmed citation in the National Archives mentions that the fort was named after Vice President George M. Dallas (who was inaugurated in 1845). The naming of the post after Commodore Dallas seems to be the more plausible case. The first troops were withdrawn the following month and reoccupied on February 5, 1839. In order to avoid the spread of disease during the hot humid Florida summers, the fort's garrison was withdrawn again in June and reoccupied on October 22, 1839. Between 1841 and 1842, Fort Dallas's garrison was made up of Companies F and G of the Eighth United States Infantry Regiment. On February 1, 1842, the fort was turned over to the navy; however, the army reoccupied the fort on October 20, 1849, and remained there until December 31, 1850. The army reoccupied the post again on January 3, 1855, at the outbreak of the Third Seminole War, commonly referred to as the "Billy Bowlegs War." The post was permanently abandoned on June 10, 1858. One of Fort Dallas's barracks, made of tabby, is preserved today in Lummus Park in downtown Miami—making it the only standing and best-preserved military frontier structure of the Seminole Wars.

Fort Dallas as it appeared at the turn of the nineteenth century.

The barracks is now preserved within Lummus Park in downtown Miami.

Fort Duncan McRee (Addison Blockhouse)

During the Second Seminole War, numerous plantations were attacked by the Seminoles. The former Carrickfergus Plantation was granted to John Addison by Spanish authorities in 1816. Many of the structures, including the kitchen, were built of coquina rock and were erected between 1807 and 1825. By 1836 the property was owned by Duncan McRae and early in that year, possibly January, the dwellings and kitchen were burned during an attack by Seminoles. The following month South Carolina militia began building earthworks around the ruins of the kitchen upon their arrival to the area. Named by the troops after the owner, the fort was garrisoned for a month and was involved in a defensive battle where three soldiers were killed. The site is now preserved in Tomoka State Park.

The Addison Blockhouse with the earthworks of Fort Duncan McRee can be reached by boat from Tomoka State Park.

FORT FOSTER

In northeastern Hillsborough County stands a re-created fort of a bygone era. There were two forts that rested upon this site during the Second Seminole War (1835–42). This site was important in that it protected a bridge over the Hillsborough River and was a vital part of the Old Fort King Military Road (segments of which are now part of U.S. 301) that went from Fort King (Ocala) to Fort Brooke (Tampa). It was on this road that Major Francis Dade and his men were massacred near Bushnell by Seminole Indians on December 28, 1835.

The first structure on the site was a trestle bridge constructed in 1828 that led the Fort King Military Road over the Hillsborough River. With ongoing hostilities by Seminoles over deportation policies, the army began to take measures to prevent or quell an uprising. Ordered to reinforce Fort King, Major Dade's relief force of artillery and infantrymen departed Fort Brooke and discovered that the bridge had been burned by the Seminoles in December 1835. The detachment spent the night near the burned bridge and forded the river the following day. The Seminoles, under the leadership of Chiefs Alligator and Jumper, attacked and massacred Major Dade and 108 of his officers and men near present-day Bushnell. This attack would throw Florida and the United States into one of the bloodiest Indian wars, the Second Seminole War.

The site proved to be of utmost importance and a fortification to protect the crossing was ordered. A fort on the site would protect the vital supply link from ambushes between Forts Brooke and King. Three companies of Alabama volunteers were sent to rebuild the bridge and construct a fort to go with the strategic bridge in March 1836. Within two days, a simple stockade fortification was constructed and named Fort Alabama. In that same month, "the newly constructed Fort Alabama was left to a detachment of Louisiana volunteers who soon came under a two-hour attack by 200 Seminoles. At least one defender was killed, and '15 to 20' Seminoles were 'supposed' dead," writes Hawes in "Lieutenant's letters tell of Fort Foster in 1830s." Another Seminole attack came upon the fort in April and again was repulsed with minor casualties.

Military life in the harsh Florida environment was difficult. During the Second Seminole War, more soldiers had died from diseases than those killed in battle. Even the soldiers in Fort Alabama weren't immune to these deadly illnesses. Therefore, on April 26, two months after the establishment of the fort, its defenders were ordered to abandon the outpost. Before evacuating, Lieutenant-Colonel William S. Foster of the Fourth Infantry and his men decided to leave a surprise for any curious Seminoles who might venture into the fort. A loaded musket, probably a variation of the model 1817 U.S. Flintlock Rifle ("Common Rifle"), was aimed into a keg filled with black powder inside the powder magazine of the fort. The trigger of the musket was tied with strings and would fire when the magazine's door opened outwardly. Not too long into the march from the fort, the volunteers heard a tremendous explosion. A few months later, an army scouting party discovered the skeletal remains of three Seminole warriors who were killed by the booby-trapped powder magazine of Fort Alabama.

As the war escalated, the abandoned site proved to be vital again. On November 28, 1836, Major General Thomas Sidney Jesup, the appointed commander for the Florida operations, ordered Lieutenant-Colonel Foster to rebuild and reinforce the recently deserted Fort Alabama and "to proceed to the site on the Withlacoochee and establish Fort Dade," according to Laumer's article "This Was Fort Dade." The new role for the site, next to protecting the bridge and the military road, was to serve as a supply depot. Within two days Colonel Foster had departed from Fort Brooke for the site with 320 men. The new fort was constructed quickly and better than the previous Fort Alabama. The fort was built with two two-story blockhouses, a powder magazine, a commissary store and a palisade around the stockade walls. A corner of the fort that faced the bridge was constructed to have a gun embrasure. This embrasure was armed with a cannon, probably a twelve-pounder mountain howitzer that would fire projectiles or shot onto the bridge when under attack by Seminoles. When the fort was sufficiently finished, Colonel Foster left a small garrison to man the outpost and continued on to construct a similar fort and bridge, Fort Dade, near present-day Dade City on the Withlacoochee River. Within three weeks, the outpost was inspected by General Jesup, who was satisfied with the manner of construction of the new fort. The general thereby named it Fort Foster.

During January 1837, the few remaining men of Colonel Foster's construction crew were replaced by navy personnel. A group of approximately fifty sailors under the command of Lieutenant Thomas L. Leib were soon under constant Seminole attack immediately after taking possession of Fort Foster. The Indians' attempt to destroy the bridge and fort failed one attack after another. Leib wrote that "it took 'the discharge of one of our field pieces and a volley of musketry' to drive off another Indian effort to burn the bridge Feb. 3. Leib gained 100 Marine reinforcements from Fort Brooke, and the attacks let up," writes Hawes in "Lieutenant's letters tell of Fort Foster in 1830s." Despite constant Indian attacks, the fort managed to conduct regular convoys of supplies along the Fort King Military Road.

Around March, news that the Seminoles had agreed to move to the south of the Hillsborough River by April (an agreement that the Seminoles had no intention of keeping) had reached Fort Foster. The outpost's next duty was to keep the Seminoles south of the Hillsborough River and the settlers to the north. Soon a contingent of the United States Second Artillery, under the command of Major R.A. Zantzinger, replaced the battle-weary sailors and marines at Fort Foster. Approximately 180 out of the assigned 305 men were actually present at the fort, due to detached service, AWOL and/or furloughs. Still, the number of men was larger than what the fort could hold within its walls. For that reason alone, many of the men slept in tents or other makeshift shelters outside the fort walls.

By April, living conditions had worsened at the fort due to overcrowding and to unhealthy marshes nearby. From these marshes came mosquitoes laden with deadly diseases that wreaked havoc upon the helpless soldiers. Cases of malaria, typhoid and dysentery were reported by the post physician, Dr. J.H. Baldwin. In his writings, Baldwin stated that "whenever it rains, the pickets are overflowed and the tents of the soldiers are flooded with water…When this is succeeded by a hot sun, new cases of dysentery and diarrhea invariably occur—some of which are very violent," writes Hawes in "Disease plagued fort during 2nd Seminole War." The doctor feared that if the illnesses couldn't be prevented, the outpost would face a possible epidemic. Both Dr. Baldwin and Major Zantzinger recomended to General Jesup that the fort be abandoned. The general followed the recommendation and all but fifty men were evacuated to a camp near Lake Thonotosassa on May 15, 1837. Eventually all the men, including the few remaining at the fort, were ordered to Fort Brooke by the beginning of June.

During the month of October, when the fall season brought forth cooler weather, the fort was able to be reoccupied under the guidance of Brevet Major Francis S. Belton. The installation continued to carry out its function as a supply depot. However, as the war progressed and the Seminoles were forced farther south into the dark swamp-laden interior of Florida, life at the fort became simpler for the soldiers. Soon a sutler was permitted by General Jesup to sell goods and conveniences, including bootleg alcohol, to the soldiers at Fort Foster and nearby Fort Dade. Though it was officially banned by the army, many soldiers managed to buy and/or make contraband alcohol for "recreational" use.

The following spring of 1838, General Jesup, before being replaced by General Zachary Taylor as commander for military operations in Florida, ordered the abandonment of Fort Foster before the coming of the summer months. In 1849, the post was briefly reactivated when it was feared that the Seminoles would bring another uprising. The site soon became forgotten and remained undisturbed for close to 130 years. The Military Road survived in use for another 100 years until U.S. 301 was paved into existence in 1934. It wasn't until the 1970s that the state began archaeological excavations and research on the former site of Fort Foster.

Based on their findings from their excavations and research, the Division of Recreation and Parks proceeded to construct an authentic reproduction of the bridge and fort on the original site in 1979. Also, a small interpretive center and museum that contains many artifacts from the state archaeological excavations in the 1970s was built nearby. Within the fort, state park rangers are dressed in the uniforms of the United States Second Artillery and therefore give the appearance of what the soldiers of the Second Seminole War must have looked like. These "soldiers" perform their duties about the fort and explain to visitors the fort's function, "their personal views of the war and the life of an artilleryman in a frontier Florida fort," according to the Fort Foster Historic Site pamphlet. Both the fort and museum are part of the Fort Foster State Historic Site within the Hillsborough River State Park near Tampa.

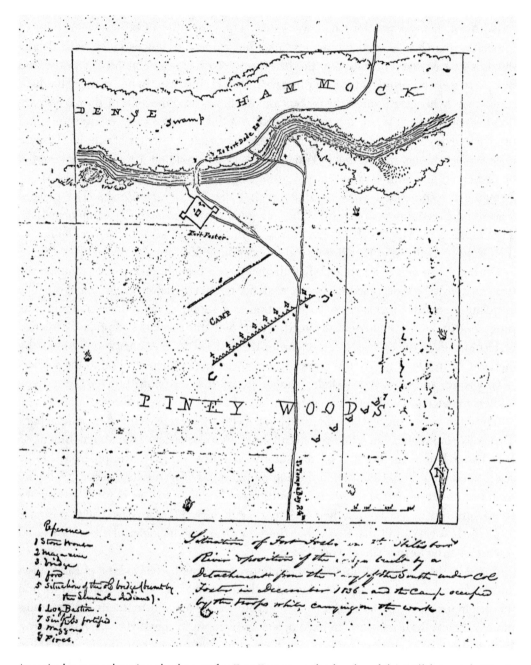

A period survey showing the layout for Fort Foster on the banks of the Hillsborough River. *Courtesy of Florida State Archives.*

A reconstructed Fort Foster as it appears today.

A view of the fort's interior as seen from the blockhouse.

From time to time living history programs depicting a soldier's life in the 1830s are displayed in Fort Foster.

Fort Foster's strategic importance was the defense of the bridge over the Hillsborough River.

Fort Gadsden

There are few reminders of the War of 1812 and the First Seminole War in Florida's history. Fort Gadsden is one such reminder that served as an active participant in both of these conflicts. Early in the fort's history, many foreign and domestic powers tried to possess the area due to its strategic importance. The fort humbly began as an English Indian trading post and ended as a remote Confederate battery on the banks of the Apalachicola River.

In 1804, an Indian trading post was established on Prospect Bluff on the banks of the Apalachicola River by James Innerarity, an agent of the firm of John Forbes and Company. Approximately thirty acres of land were ceded to the company after a conference between the Indians and the company's representatives, which was administered under the Spanish governor of West Florida, Vizente Folch y Juan. A dwelling, a storehouse, a granary and a few other buildings were built within three years after the company's acquisition of the land. Business at the new post was soon to be seen as a losing venture and the company talked of withdrawing from the area. However, the British military began to see the strategic importance of the failing Indian trading post.

After the loss of the North American colonies during the Revolutionary War, the British military felt that their disgrace should be avenged. The Apalachicola River proved to be of importance in that the river leads into the state of Georgia. Also of importance were the Creek nations that inhabit the areas near the river. The English government believed that by sending British agents into the area where the trading post was located, they could gather support and sympathy from the nearby Indians and "promote unrest and hostility among the Indians on the American frontiers," writes Boyd in "Events at Prospect Bluff on the Apalachicola River, 1808–1818." Next to stirring the Indians in the American states and territories, the British further planned to harass American commerce in foreign ports. In order to erect a British outpost in the area, western Florida had to be taken by force.

With the outbreak of the War of 1812, President Madison feared that British forces might invade the North American continent by seizing East Florida. Therefore, the American president ordered that United States troops should take and hold the western part of East Florida. On April 15, 1813, American troops took possession of Mobile, now within the modern state of Alabama, and established Fort Bowyer in the Mobile Bay area. It wasn't until the summer of 1814 that British troops made an attempt to seize western Florida. At the mouth of the Apalachicola Bay, approximately three hundred British soldiers and their officers landed on St. Georges Island. These troops consisted of various units of Royal Marines and of West India regiments. Their mission was to establish a fort on the banks of the Apalachicola River within the Spanish territory of East Florida.

British troops were able to take possession of certain areas in East Florida without Spanish interference. This was due to the weakness of the Spanish colonial forces in

Florida and the devastating war between Napoleonic and British forces in the Iberian peninsula of Spain. The Spaniards were also reluctant allies in that the English had ousted Napoleon's relative from the Spanish throne and re-established the legitimate Spanish monarchy. Even with its re-establishment to the throne, the Spanish crown never really had any impact on civil authority in the colonies of the New World.

Within weeks of the arrival of English troops, Indians and escaped black slaves were being recruited and trained militarily for war against the United States. The British wasted no time in training the Indians "to fire a swivel, sound the war whoop, fire three or four rounds of small arms, sound (carry) the war whoop to every village who repeated it and are ready to march on the shortest notice," writes Boyd in "Events at Prospect Bluff on the Apalachicola River, 1808–1818." Some of these Indians soon began to send out raiding parties into Georgia. The trading post was to serve as a "store" for the five thousand guns and its supplies of ammunition that the English soldiers had brought with them. In fact, this "store" was to be a fortification that would bear its guns down on any enemy forces that might venture unto the dark waters of the Apalachicola River.

Edward Nicholls, a colonel of artillery, was instructed to build a fort approximately twenty miles north from the mouth of the Apalachicola River and to furnish the fortification with artillery and ammunition. The fort was situated on a low bluff of the eastern bank of the river. The fort's construction "consisted of an octagonal central earth work located about five hundred feet from the river bank, evidently the principal magazine, and was surrounded by an extensive rectangular enclosure covering about seven acres with bastions on the eastern corners having parapets fifteen feet high and eighteen feet thick," writes Boyd in "Events at Prospect Bluff on the Apalachicola River, 1808–1818." By the time in which the fort was completed, the War of 1812 had ended with the battle of New Orleans and the Treaty of Ghent in the spring of 1815. British troops were ordered to leave Florida by the beginning of the summer.

For a short time, Colonel Nicholls remained at the newly constructed fort after his troops had departed to Pensacola. He was to supervise the transition of command to the black and Indian forces that were trained during Nicholls's stay in the area. The new occupants of the fort were grateful for the military supplies and pieces of artillery that were left behind by the departing British. These supplies and weapons enabled the Indians to defend the river from American encroachment into the area and to commence attacks upon American settlers across the Georgia border. The United States had learned of the transaction of the fort to the British allies and decided that the fort must be destroyed. The Americans named the hostile outpost the Negro Fort.

In late April of 1816, Secretary of War General Andrew Jackson sent an emissary to the Spanish governor in Pensacola demanding the abandonment of the Negro Fort. The demand also stated that the escaped black slaves must be returned to their American owners across the border in Georgia. The emissary also noted to the Spanish governor that if the Spaniards were unable to handle this problem, the United States would handle it themselves. "In reply Governor Zuniga disclaimed responsibility for the presence of the fort, stated that the Spanish negroes at any rate, were regarded as rebels, but that he would be unable to act against them until authorized by the Captain General," reports Boyd in "Events at Prospect Bluff on the Apalachicola River, 1808–1818." On his return trip to Washington, the emissary had reported that in addition to the escaped black slaves that were in the fort there were also a few Choctaws, Upper Creeks and Seminoles. Even before Jackson sent an emissary to the Spanish authorities in East Florida, he ordered General Gaines to prepare an attack on the Negro Fort.

Lieutenant Colonel Duncan L. Clinch, under orders by General Gaines, constructed Fort Scott on the Georgia-Florida border upon the banks of the Flint River in June of 1816. This fort was to serve as a supply depot for operations along the Apalachicola River and against the Negro Fort. The navy was also directed to send one or two of their gunboats to protect the supply ships heading toward Fort Scott along the Apalachicola River. The combined army-navy force was ordered to destroy the Negro Fort if any opposition was met. When the emissary returned from East Florida, Jackson ordered that the fort must be immediately destroyed.

Commodore Patterson, who had commanded the New Orleans Naval Station, ordered "that gunboats 149 and 154 meet the schooner transports *Semilante* and *General Pike* carrying the supplies for Camp Crawford [Fort Scott] at Pass Christian, and convoy them to their destination, with orders to co-operate with the military force in the event opposition should be encountered from the negro fort," reports Boyd in "Events at Prospect Bluff on the Apalachicola River, 1808–1818." The naval force, under the command of L. Loomis, had departed from New Orleans on June 19, 1816, and arrived at the mouth of the Apalachicola River on July 10. From there the force joined up with some detachments of Colonel Clinch's force. After learning of Loomis's arrival, Colonel Clinch and 116 of his men from elements of the Fourth and Seventh U.S. Infantry Regiments descended down the river to meet the naval force on July 17.

Within three days the forces of Colonel Clinch and sailing master Loomis were united in an area near the hostile fort. A force of 150 friendly Indians, under the command of Major John McIntosh, were to surround the fort and engage it with artillery duels. Three days earlier, on July 17, Loomis's foraging party had been ambushed. One seaman survived, three were killed and one was captured by the Indians. The captured seaman, Edward Daniels, was taken to the fort where he was tarred and burnt alive by his black and Indian captors. Some of Clinch's men apprehended an Indian bearing the scalp of one of the members of the foraging party a few days later. The Indian was summarily executed after his interrogation.

The hostile actions taken by the defenders of the fort had proven to Colonel Clinch that the fort must be destroyed. A small battery was erected opposite from the fort's shores in order to assist the gunboats in their attack upon the Negro Fort. But Loomis viewed the battery as ineffective and he stated that the gunboats could handle the attack without the battery. Loomis's force sailed into position at 5:00 a.m. on July 27 and the fort's inhabitants began firing their cannons upon the American force; the Americans replied with shots from the gunboat's thirty-two-pounder cannons. The first rounds were of cold shot, to determine the range, and afterward hot shots were used. The first hot shot, fired from gunboat 154, penetrated and exploded the magazine within the Negro Fort. The explosion blew the fort apart and left a mound that was "about one hundred feet in diameter and several feet high, and was surrounded by a trench," reported Griffin in "An Archeologist at Fort Gadsden."

When the American force rushed into the interior of the fort, there was no resistance. The explosion killed 270 of the 300 defenders of the fort. The dismembered bodies of the inhabitants lay scattered about the fort and its immediate area. Of those that survived were the fort's commandant, an escaped black slave called Garson, and an Indian chief. Both were executed on the spot once Colonel Clinch learned of the fate of seaman Daniels.

The Americans also found a large cache of weapons and supplies that the British had left behind. Of the inventory made after the short battle, there were "four twenty-four-pound cannons, four six-pound cannons, beside a field piece and howitzer. In addition there were found twenty-five hundred stands of muskets with accoutrements, five hundred carbines and five hundred swords," writes Boyd in "Events at Prospect Bluff on the Apalachicola River, 1808–1818." The Americans believed that within the magazine were about "three hundred quarter-casks of rifle powder and one hundred sixty-two barrels of cannon powder, besides other stores and clothing," continues Boyd.

The combined army-navy force departed from the remnants of the Negro Fort after setting fire to the remaining structures on August 3. Two days after the destruction of the fort, a Spanish task force, under Don Benigno Garcia Calderon, arrived in attempt to destroy the Negro Fort. Finding out that they were too late, Benigno confronted Loomis's gunboats and demanded that all captured weapons and supplies be handed over to the Spanish authorities. Loomis refused and sailed toward homeport due to the Spaniards' inability to enforce their demands. The destruction of the fort had left a vacuum in which American traders were now competing with British traders, notably the John Forbes & Co., along the Apalachicola River area. By the fall of 1816, Fort Scott was evacuated and its troops were sent to Fort Gaines and other military installations.

For two years the site of the Negro Fort was left to the growing Florida foliage. Due to increasing Indian troubles along the Florida-Georgia border, U.S. troops were ordered to reoccupy Fort Scott in the summer of 1817. During November 1817, a supply force of three vessels was attacked during its journey from Fort Montgomery to Fort Scott along the Apalachicola River. The supply vessels finally arrived at Fort Scott in mid-January after being delayed by the ongoing attacks by the Indians along the river's shores. With these rising Indian problems, the War Department gave permission to the post commander at Fort Scott, General Edmund Gaines, to cross into Spanish Florida and seize or punish those Indians responsible, but to leave any Spanish military outposts alone. General Andrew Jackson, a well-known Indian fighter, was called into service and through his actions would begin the First Seminole War.

General Jackson arrived at Fort Scott with a large contingent of Georgia and Tennessee militiamen in early March 1818. The force, including Fort Scott's garrison troops of the Fourth and Seventh U.S. Infantry Regiments, totaled close to two thousand men. However, provisions for these men could not last for more than three days. With the low amount of provisions at the fort, Jackson decided to meet the next scheduled supply vessels at the mouth of the Apalachicola River with his troops. The campaign began with Jackson's force departing Fort Scott on March 10, 1818. Within six days, the force was encamped at the former site of the Negro Fort on Prospect Bluff.

The site at Prospect Bluff had impressed the general for its strategic importance and he ordered an army engineer, Lieutenant James Gadsden, to rebuild the fort. The new fort was to serve as a supply depot and was to guard the supply lines on the Apalachicola River. Within the grounds of the Negro Fort a smaller stockade fort with surrounding earthworks and palisades was constructed. The fort's outline was a star-shaped pattern, which was a common design found in America's first system of fortifications. The large eastern bastions of the old English fort, believed to be fifteen feet high and eighteen feet thick, were probably leveled by the Americans so as to prevent future attackers from using these works and to permit greater visibility from the small fort.

Lieutenant Gadsden wrote in his report "The Defenses of the Floridas" that the fort was "a temporary work, hastily erected, and of perishable materials, without constant repairs it could not last more than four or five years. If the position should therefore be selected for a permanent defence, an entire new work will have to be constructed." General Jackson was very well pleased with the finished fort and named it Fort Gadsden in honor of the engineer who had constructed it. During the short campaigns of the First Seminole War, American troops would garrison the fort within the Spanish territory of Florida.

Upon hearing that large concentrations of Indians were in the vicinity of Pensacola and St. Marks in early May, General Jackson decided to seize these Spanish outposts. After leaving a strong garrison in Fort Gadsden, the general proceeded to capture the Spanish forts in Pensacola and in St. Marks. "In his seizure of the Spanish posts at St. Marks and Pensacola, Jackson appears to have exercised his own convictions and judgement, and in doing so exceeded the orders received from the War Department," writes Boyd in "Events at Prospect Bluff on the Apalachicola River, 1808–1818." It wasn't until August that the president of the United States ordered all properties seized by American troops be returned to the proper Spanish authorities. However, Fort Gadsden was to remain in American hands to ensure the safety of American interests in the Apalachicola River area.

The fort remained in active use until the cession of Florida in 1821. On July 22, 1821, Major Fanning was instructed by General Jackson to abandon Fort Gadsden and occupy the former Spanish Fort San Marcos de Apalache. After Florida was ceded to the

United States, a town site called Colinton was established outside of the fort's confines. The town's future was doomed to extinction with the establishment of the seaport town of Apalachicola at the mouth of the river of that same name. The site of Fort Gadsden remained unmolested for forty years until the outbreak of the War Between the States in 1861.

By the eve of the Civil War, the town of Apalachicola was the largest exporting and importing port in Florida. The river was the "breadbasket of the South" for the river and its tributaries led into the states of Alabama, Florida and Georgia. Knowing of the strategic importance of the area, General Robert E. Lee dispatched a letter to General James H. Trapier (recorded by Dowdey and Manarin in *The Wartime Papers of Robert E. Lee*), in which Lee recommended that

> *the only troops to be retained in Florida are such as may be necessary to defend the Apalachicola River, by which the enemy's gunboats may penetrate far into the state of Georgia. You are therefore desired to put that river & harbor in a satisfactory state of defense, & send forward all troops not necessary for that purpose to report to Genl. A.S. Johnston.*

Based upon the recommendations of General Lee, the newly formed army of the Confederate States of America re-occupied Fort Gadsden early in the year of 1862.

During the Confederate occupation of the fort, a four-gun battery was erected on the fort site and detachments of cavalry and infantry were sent to man the strategic area. Apparently, no structural remodeling of the fort was done by the troops stationed there. The only event of the war that occurred in the near vicinity was a Union raid on May 25, 1863. A Federal gunboat bypassed the Confederate's obstructions in the river and seized, not too far from the fort, a small vessel containing fifty bales of cotton. Fort Gadsden was finally abandoned around July 1863, when its troops were contracting malaria.

The fort's site remained forgotten and overgrown with brushes and trees until it became part of the Apalachicola National Forest. The federal government granted the Florida Board of Parks and Recreation close to seventy-eight acres of land for maintenance as a state historic site in 1961. The historic earthworks of the English, Negro and American forts are still visible and well preserved today. One can still see the crater left by the explosion of the Negro Fort's magazine in 1816, as well as the numerous shallow depressions marking the resting places at the nearby Renegade cemetery of those killed in that terrible explosion. An outdoor museum is located near the fort and contains a miniature model of Fort Gadsden along with various artifacts uncovered at the fort.

A model showing Fort Gadsden as it appeared during the War of 1812.

The earthworks of Fort Gadsden are well preserved.

Fort King

The fort stood on a nearby knoll and was built in 1827 adjacent to a Seminole agency. A stockade was erected and enclosed by a barricade of split logs that stood twenty feet tall. On one corner a fourteen-foot-square blockhouse was constructed and other buildings included a magazine, two kitchens and quarters for enlisted men and officers and storage buildings. The stockade enclosed an area of 162 by 152 feet. Heavy timbered gates were placed in the two sides of the stockade. The enlisted men's barracks were divided into four 25-foot-square compartments, while the officers' quarters consisted of two separate buildings, each being about 20 by 50 feet. The fort was originally built and garrisoned by two companies of the Fourth U.S. Infantry Regiment from February 1827 to July 1829, when they were ordered to abandon Fort King. The fort was occupied by United States troops and militia on and off for the next seventeen years.

Fort King was reoccupied in 1832 when plans were formulated to "convince" the Indians to emigrate to a new reservation in the West. Outside its stockade, on December 28, 1835, warriors led by Osceola ambushed and murdered General Wiley Thompson and four others. That same day, troops marching to the fort's relief perished in the Dade's Massacare, thus beginning the Second Seminole War. After the Seminole War ended, the last troops abandoned the fort on March 25, 1843, and Fort King became the temporary seat of newly created Marion County in 1844. In 1845 the government granted permission for the soldiers' quarters to be used as a temporary courthouse. When the Circuit Court moved to its newly constructed courthouse in September 1846, the fort was salvaged for building materials for construction in Ocala the following month. The fort site was later purchased by the McCall family.

In 1927 the first of three attempts to preserve the fort site began when the Daughters of the American Revolution purchased a lot that was once the post cemetery. By 2001 a combined effort consisting of the city of Ocala, Marion County and the State of Florida acquired the final parcel of land, about thirty-seven acres, on which the fort once stood. In 2004 the Fort King site was designated as a national landmark and there are plans to turn the site over to the National Park Service, thereby preserving one of the most important military outposts during the removal of the Florida Indians.

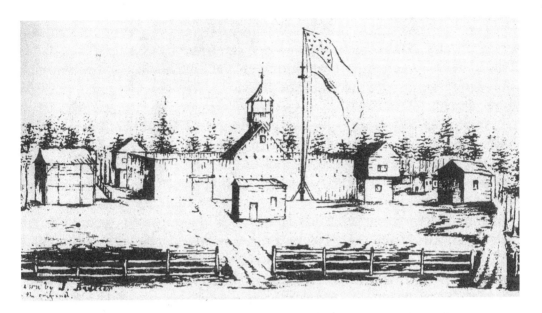

Fort King as it appeared during the Second Seminole War. *Courtesy of Florida State Archives.*

A portion of the Fort King military cemetery has been preserved as a park.

The hill behind the historical marker of Fort King was purchased by city, county and state government agencies with the aim of preserving the entire fort site.

The history of Fort King and artifacts from the site are preserved within the Marion County Museum of History. *Courtesy of Marion County Museum of History, photo by author.*

Fort Myers

Fort Myers was born out of the chaos of the Second Seminole War. After Major Dade and his command were massacred near Bushnell on December 28, 1835, a war was raged throughout Florida for nearly six years. This war would cost the lives of 1,466 federal troops and several hundred Florida and Georgia militia volunteers. After the Seminole War of 1836–42, the army felt that more forts were needed in case the Indians were to rise up once more. Thus began the history of Fort Myers.

Fort Myers was erected upon the ruins of Fort Harvie by Major Ridgely on Wednesday, February 20, 1850. Two days prior, the major had sailed from Fort Brooke with two companies of artillery upon orders from Major General Twiggs. Early in the morning of the twentieth, Major Ridgely and his men sailed up the Caloosahatchee. "Fifteen miles up the river Major Ridgely spied the ruins of Fort Harvie. Major Ridgely landed and looked the site over. He found that the buildings which had been erected there in the winter of 1841–1842 had been almost completely destroyed by fires, probably set by revengeful Indians," writes Grismer in *The Story of Fort Myers*.

The name of Fort Myers was ordered by Major General Twiggs to be placed upon the new outpost on the Caloosahatchee River. The fort was named after Colonel Abraham C. Meyers, chief quartermaster of the Department of Florida and husband to General Twiggs's daughter. Within a few weeks of the fort's founding, men and supplies were coming up the Caloosahatchee River to build and garrison the fort. At first many of the structures were makeshift and it would take a year for the establishment of any permanent structures in the new outpost.

Indians began appearing almost immediately after the fort's establishment. "Billy Bowlegs was one of the first arrivals. He was friendly and talked freely with Major Ridgely. He said that the Seminoles had established a number of settlements in the Big Cypress about thirty miles southeast of the camp and had planted gardens. They were satisfied with their new homes, he said, and wanted nothing more than to be left alone," writes Grismer. This cordiality would not last for long, for Indian hate was brewing again in the Florida territory and in Washington, D.C. Also, the Indians felt very uncomfortable about a military outpost in the middle of what they believed to be an Indian reservation.

The new fort quickly brought a building boom to the area and a town would soon form around the military installation. Materials such as bricks and other permanent building supplies were sent from Pensacola to further strengthen the outpost. However, questions were raised about large sums of government money that were spent on the fort during the 1850s; an investigation was ordered by the War Department. "Major J. McKinstry went to the fort in April, 1856, and, after a thorough probe, reported that in his opinion 'unnecessarily expensive buildings have been erected and that a lavish and uncalled for expenditure of public money has [been] obtained at that post, particularly for the hospital building,'" reports Grismer. In his report, he showed detailed drawings of at least fifty-seven buildings. But what probably irked the major was the construction of a bowling alley and a bathing pier on the Caloosahatchee River. By 1854, the fort was considered one of Florida's finest for its extravagant luxuries. During the first half of the decade life at the fort was peaceful.

At all costs, soldiers were ordered not to harass the local Indians. The memories of the bloody and costly Second Seminole War were still fresh in the minds of some military and government officials. However, both the federal government and the State of Florida desired Indian removal from the territories. But the question was, *how*. A special Indian agent, Luther Blake, was sent to Florida in April 1851. He managed to bring a few Indian leaders, including Billy Bowlegs, to see the north, but nothing came of the trip. With no success and a costly government bill for Blake's expenses, the Indian agent was replaced with Captain John C. Casey in 1853. Casey devised a plan in which the Indians would be forced into a war with the United States. The plan was submitted to Jefferson Davis, the new secretary of war, and was approved.

"The first phase of the plan provided for cutting off the Seminoles from all sources of supplies. Trading posts were to be closed and the Indians were to be prevented from entering settlements anywhere on the East Coast or on the keys. Nowhere were they to be permitted to obtain provisions or ammunition," writes Grismer. The second part of the plan called for forts from the Second Seminole War, such as Denuad, Thompson and Center, to be reactivated. Also, troops were to encircle and push the Seminoles into a tighter and smaller area. Next to this, surveying parties from the War Department's Topographical Engineers were to be ordered into Seminole territory. Therefore, the Indians would be incited into a war and the United States would then have reason to expel them from their lands.

A surveying party, under Lieutenant George L. Hartsuff, left Fort Myers for Big Cypress within Indian territory. On December 19, 1855, the surveying crew ran across a garden belonging to Billy Bowlegs. The crew, knowing the owner of the garden, promptly began destroying the garden. When Bowlegs returned and found what had happened, he demanded compensation. The crew "tripped Billy and sent him sprawling. When he arose, his face was covered with dirt. Then the whole camp roared. Seething with anger, Billy left," reports Grismer. A day later, Billy returned with a few of his warriors and attacked Hartsuff's camp. Of eleven of the crew, four were wounded, including Hartsuff, and two killed. A third war with the Seminoles had begun and the conflict would be known as Billy Bowleg's War.

This war lasted from December 1855 to the spring of 1858 and brought economic growth in central and southern Florida to a virtual standstill. The soldiers outnumbered the Indians by fourteen to one, in that "there were 800 federal troops stationed in South Florida; 260 state troops in federal service; and 400 troops in state service. Opposing this force of 1,460 men were about 100 Seminole warriors," writes Covington in his essay "An Episode in the Third Seminole War." Unlike the spectacles of the Second Seminole War, the Third Seminole War consisted of a few minor engagements and skirmishes. But the soldiers' task in apprehending the Indians was further made difficult because the Indians were able to implement guerilla warfare tactics in the Florida swamps.

The soldiers at Fort Myers faced the fear of ambushes when any excursions from the post were made. Scouting parties and supply trains were ambushed by the Seminoles and before the soldiers could return fire, the Indians would be gone. One officer who knew that the army could not win a war when the enemy did not follow conventional rules was General William S. Harney. General Harney, a veteran from the previous Seminole war, proposed that the only way to defeat the Seminoles was to destroy their hideouts, burn their crops and kill or capture any Seminoles (women, children and warriors). He also proposed that the job could be done with good results by using Florida volunteers who were well suited to the environment of Florida. The military accepted the proposal and to ensure enlistment, the military offered rewards for the capture of Indian women and children and a higher reward for warriors.

Three boat companies, consisting of forty-five men each, of Florida volunteers were formed in 1857. These men ventured into the Glades in long flat-bottomed boats and faced extreme hardships in search for hostile Indians. Their military records were of successes and failures. By the end of the year after their formation, the volunteers managed to capture no more than thirty warriors. However, the Seminole uprising was becoming too costly for those who had waged it; peace was near in 1858.

The bloodied Seminole warriors and their families, under the leadership of Billy Bowlegs, were being induced by their Creek and Seminole relatives to join them in the Arkansas reservation. Colonel Elias Rector, the superintendent of Indian affairs in the Arkansas reservation, arrived at Fort Myers with forty-six Creeks and Seminoles in February 1858. Billy Bowlegs arrived a few weeks later to negotiate with Rector. After shrewdly bargaining, Billy Bowlegs managed to get for his warriors a substantial sum of money for losses suffered during the short but bloody war. The proposals were accepted by some of his people and within three weeks small groups of Indians were appearing at the fort.

Close to 124 Indians were exiled from their Florida home. On May 4, 1858, the Seminoles were transported from Florida by transport ships to Arkansas. Only 350 Seminoles remained in Florida; these were the undefeated. With the war over, Fort Myers was abandoned during June 1858.

The outpost remained in disuse until the advent of the War Between the States. When Florida seceded from the Union on January 10, 1861, only three major fortifications and ports remained in Federal hands in Florida: Fort Pickens in Pensacola, Fort Taylor in Key West and Fort Jefferson in the Dry Tortugas. The state became a major supplier in cattle prior to the war and after secession supplied beef for the Confederate States of America. The Federals planned to harass this supply link and therefore needed a location to stage raids into the interior of the state from a coastal point. Also, the captured beef fed the Union garrison in Key West and the Union naval blockading squadrons lurking along the coasts of Florida. As early as January 1861, the Federals were looking to start a base in Fort Myers, well into the Rebel heartland.

The old fort's location was ideal for Federals looking for recruits because it was reported that large numbers of Union sympathizers were living in southern Florida. At the outset of the war, some of these south Floridians had gone to Key West and formed a company known as the Florida Rangers. In late December 1863, four and a half years after the abandonment of Fort Myers, a small company of Florida Rangers and five companies of Federal troops reoccupied the old fort.

The Federal soldiers were surprised that the fort and its buildings were still in excellent shape after all those years of disuse in the Florida climate. The fort was further strengthened through the construction of earthworks. "It was about fifteen feet wide at the base and seven feet high and extended in the shape of a crescent from the eastern edge of the hospital grounds to about five hundred feet below the wharf. This would be from near the present Edison bridge to about the present Monroe Street," writes Grismer. A large barracks was also constructed within the following few months in 1864. Soon, the fort was prepared for any Confederate attacks and was ready to commence cattle raids into the interior of Florida.

The cattle raids made by the Federals from Fort Myers became quite profitable for the Union. It is estimated that close to five thousand heads of cattle were captured between January 1864 and April 1865 by Northern raiding parties. Due to the frequency and success of these raids, many settlers were forced to organize a home guard militia unit to combat the Union threat by the end of 1864. Nine companies were formed under the name of the Cattle Guard Battalion, usually referred to as the "Cow Cavalry," and were under the command of Colonel Charles J. Munnerlyn. Confederate officials began to see that the Federal fort must be taken at all costs. As early as April 1864, Lieutenant-Colonel T.W. Brevard of the Sixty-fourth Georgia Regiment was ordered into the Fort Meade district to capture Confederate deserters and "to seize Fort Myers if in his opinion it could be taken, but he was primarily to protect the cattle supply from further depredation," Johns writes in *Florida During the Civil War*. It wasn't until February 21, 1865, that a Confederate attempt to capture the Federal fort would be made.

Munnerlyn's 275 men of the Cattle Guard Battalion and a cannon, commanded by Major William Footman, began attacking the Federal post of Fort Myers. The Union soldiers replied with three of their own cannons. After an entire day of exchanging cannon and musket fire, the Confederate soldiers figured that the fort could not be taken easily from combat-experienced Federal troops. Davis writes in *The Civil War and Reconstruction in Florida* that Captain J. Doyle reported only "nine Federal pickets are captured and one picket is killed. Some of the cattle of the Fort Meyers garrison are driven off." To note, there were black troops, namely some companies from the prestigious Second United States Colored Infantry, stationed at Fort Myers who had distinguished themselves quite well under enemy fire. A war correspondent, present at the time of the Confederate attack on Fort Myers, stated that the black soldiers

The blockhouse of Fort Myers as it appeared in the October 6, 1858 issue of *Frank Leslie's Illustrated Newspaper*.

"were in the thickest of the fight and could hardly be restrained; they seemed totally unconcerned of danger and the constant cry was 'to get at them,'" writes Davis.

The Union victory would be the last major excitement that Federal soldiers would share at Fort Myers. For within a month after the battle, the Confederacy would end its four-year existence with Lee's surrender at Appomattox. Close to two months after the end of the war, around June 1865, Fort Myers was abandoned by the Federal troops stationed there. The outpost soon became vandalized by settlers and looters. However, within a year a town would rise up from where the old fort had stood. Fort Myers would again flourish like the phoenix.

A diorama in the Southwest Florida Museum of History showing the area covered by the military reservation. The blockhouse in the distance would have protected the main entrance to the fort's enclosure. *Courtesy of Southwest Florida Museum of History, photo by author.*

One of the most impressive memorials related to Fort Myers is that of the Second United States Colored Infantry Regiment, who were responsible for the defense of Fort Myers during the Civil War. This memorial is located in Centennial Park. Another marker related to the fort is located on the grounds of the Federal Building on Second Street.

Another model showing how the blockhouse appeared at the time of the Civil War. *Courtesy of Southwest Florida Museum of History, photo by author.*

Fort Chokonikla

Work began on October 26, 1849, on an elevated spot of ground near present-day Bowling Green. This was in response to an attack by Seminoles on the Kennedy-Darling trade store on July 17, 1849. The attack killed two whites, whose graves can still be seen today. The fort took its name from the name of the store, which had come to be known as "Chokonikla," a variant spelling of the Indian word for "burned house." No fighting occurred at the fort (consisting of three blockhouses), although a number of men died from disease. Sickness, particularly malaria and fever, were constant problems and ultimately caused the fort to be abandoned in July 1850. As many as 223 men, including a regimental band, were garrisoned at the fort at one time, but usually the number was smaller. The area is now the Paynes Creek State Historic Site.

A model showing the construction of Fort Chokonikla in 1849. *Courtesy of Paynes Creek Historic State Park, photo by author.*

A marker showing the site of one of the three blockhouses of Fort Chokonikla.

The graves of Captain George Paynes and Dempsey Whiddon, who were ambushed by Seminoles on July 17, 1849, are the only remaining link to the trading post and Fort Chokonikla.

An excellent museum depicting the history of the trading post and Fort Chokonikla can be found next to the site. *Courtesy of Paynes Creek Historic State Park, photo by author.*

Fort Harrison

According to the records of the War Department of the United States, Fort Harrison, formerly Clearwater Harbor, Florida, was established April 2, 1841. It was located at latitude twenty-eight about thirty miles west of Fort Brooke and stood on a pine bluff twenty-five feet above sea level, fronting on a bay between two and three miles wide. From two to seven companies of the Sixth United States Infantry were stationed at the post during its occupancy under command of Lieutenant-Colonel Gustavus Loomis of that regiment. That command moved to Fort Brooke about October 20, 1841. The greatest number of troops shown to have occupied the fort appears to be 20 officers and 476 enlisted men in May 1841. Besides Colonel Gustavus Dorr, and Captain George Andrews, officers of the Sixth U.S. Infantry are shown to have been stationed at the fort at various times. Fort Harrison was abandoned about November 1, 1841. Now in a residential area in Clearwater, there exists a historical marker of the fort site at 800 Druid Road.

Fort Harrison is marked by a historical marker located at 800 Druid Road in Clearwater.

The majority of Seminole War–era forts are gone and left no traces of their existence, with the exception of various historical markers that denote their approximate sites. Seen are markers for Forts Carroll, Dade, Mellon and Fraser.

Chapter Three
THE CIVIL WAR

FORT BARRANCAS

Situated on the high ground overlooking the old Spanish Battery San Antonio and Pensacola Bay stands Fort Barrancas. With the selection of Pensacola Bay as the site for a new navy yard in the mid-1820s, the Army Corps of Engineers designed and built Fort Barrancas (construction began in 1840 and ended with the completion of the fort in 1844) and its redoubt (construction began in 1845 and continued intermittently until the Civil War, and nothing more was done after 1879) in order to defend the open end of the peninsula upon which the naval yard was sited. The work was designed by Chief Engineer Joseph G. Totten under the close supervision of Captain William H. Chase, who was the onsite architect and engineer. The fort was composed of masses of earth and masonry (six million bricks were bought locally for about $10 per thousand) and included an innovative system of connecting interior vaults to sustain the central sand and earth fill, reports Parsons in his guide "Fort Barrancas and Water Battery." The cost of the work was approximately $330,000.

"Fort Barrancas was constructed to house thirty-three barbette guns and eight flanking howitzers," write the Colemans in *Guardians on the Gulf: Pensacola Fortifications, 1698–1980*. However, with the outbreak of the Civil War, the fort was only armed with thirteen eight-inch Columbiads and howitzers plus two ten-inch mortars and some smaller caliber cannons. Immediately after Florida had seceded from the Union, the Confederate Army took command of the fort and found that most of the guns had been moved to Fort Pickens on Santa Rosa Island while others were spiked when the Federal troops abandoned Fort Barrancas. The Confederacy began to strengthen its defenses by adding auxiliary batteries along the coast, thus holding a four-mile-long fortified position stretching from Fort McRee to the navy yard. All that remained under Federal control in the Pensacola area was Fort Pickens. Most of the Southern fortifications were occupied by state militias two or three months before Fort Sumter was fired upon. The three forts that remained in Federal hands in the South were Fort Taylor (Key West), Fort Jefferson (Garden Key, Dry Tortugas) and Fort Pickens (Pensacola), all in Florida.

The only time Fort Barrancas came under fire during the war was on November 22–23, 1861, as Confederate artillery at Fort Barrancas and several other positions along the main coastline exchanged artillery fire with Federal troops at Fort Pickens. Neither side suffered extensively, except that Fort Barrancas had its flagstaff shot away and its walls slightly scarred, and fires forced the Confederates to temporarily abandon Fort McRee. "A second bombardment on January 1, 1862, was equally ineffective in driving the antagonists from their defenses. In May 1862 the Confederates pulled out of Pensacola to strengthen other field armies and Union forces re-occupied all the harbor installations," writes Parsons. Though there were some repeated threats and sorties by Confederate cavalry operating out of Alabama, the fort remained in Union hands throughout the remainder of the war.

After the war ended in 1865 the few guns that remained in Fort Barrancas were maintained as part of the Coast Artillery (CA) installations. By 1900 the fort was being used to store powder, cannons and other equipment for the garrison at the post of Fort Barrancas. By 1947 all armament had been removed, according to the Colemans.

Declared obsolete as a military installation in 1947, Fort Barrancas and the old Spanish Battery San Antonio were restored by the National Park Service in 1978–80 at a cost of about $1,200,000. Today the forts are maintained by Gulf Islands National Seashore and are open to the public.

Bateria de San Antonio de Barrancas as seen from Fort Barrancas at the time of the outbreak of the Civil War.

Upon Florida's secession from the Union, Florida state troops took possession of Pensacola's defenses, with the exception of Fort Pickens.

Gunners taking aim at Fort Pickens from Fort Barrancas.

Between Fort Barrancas and the Pensacola Naval Yard there were numerous sand batteries with artillery of all types.

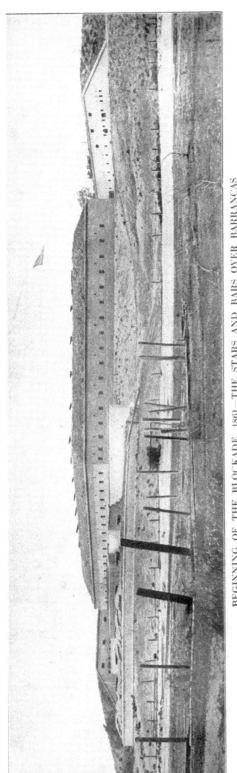

BEGINNING OF THE BLOCKADE, 1861—THE STARS AND BARS OVER BARRANCAS

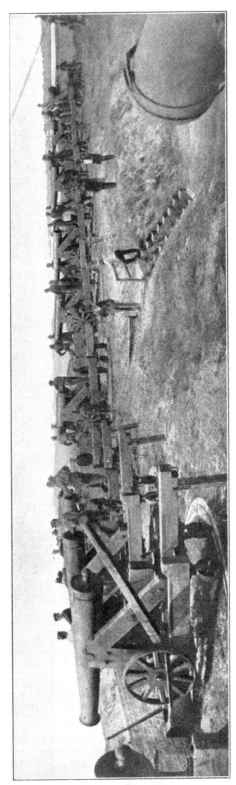

Fort Barrancas as it appeared from the beach.

An artillery duel occurred between the Confederates and the Union garrison in Fort Pickens on November 22–23, 1861.

A Confederate standard bearer proudly showing the colors of the Confederate States of America.

These sand batteries were built in varying styles, such as the one seen here.

Some guns were removed from Fort Barrancas in order to outfit the sand batteries as well as other defenses, such as Fort Walton.

The same entrance as it appears today.

The ramparts as they appear today at Fort Barrancas.

The sally port of the Advanced Redoubt.

The Advanced Redoubt for Fort Barrancas. Courtesy of National Park Service.

Battery Bluff

A Confederate battery was built early in the summer of 1863 to protect the Apalachicola River against Union gunboats. The battery consisted of two thirty-two-pounders, one twenty-four-pounder and three eighteen-pounders. All were smoothbore type and were mounted on raised firing platforms. Battery Bluff was garrisoned by Companies B and D of the Twenty-eighth Georgia Battalion, Heavy Artillery, commanded by Major Bonaud. The garrison was hastily transferred to Ocean Pond (Olustee) where on February 20, 1864, it participated in the battle of Ocean Pond, a notable Confederate victory. Scant traces of the Confederate six-gun pit on Neals Bluff (Battery Bluff) are preserved in Torreya State Park.

Scant traces of a Confederate six-gun pit on Neals Bluff ("Battery Bluff"), Torreya State Park.

FORT CLINCH

Fort Clinch is one of many masonry forts that are found along the coast of Florida. Many of these forts were started early in the nineteenth century and were actually used at the time of the War Between the States. Fort Clinch rests on the northern tip of Amelia Island and is one of many fortifications that have existed on that island from colonial times to the present.

Construction of Fort Clinch began in 1847 near the Florida-Georgia boundary. The fort was based on the third system of fortification and was similar in design to Fort Pulaski on Tybee Island, Georgia. The pentagonal fort was designed to protect the entrance of St. Mary's River, which led to the Cumberland Sound, and the port of Fernandina, Florida. The installation was named after a well-known Indian fighter from Florida's Seminole Wars, General Duncan Lamont Clinch.

Due to lack of manpower and funds the fort's construction was slow. At the outbreak of the War Between the States in 1861, only two of the three bastions were completed. "The only erected walls ran between the north and the east and north and northwest bastions. The ramparts had been installed, and the guardhouse and prison had been completed. The lumber sheds, storehouse and kitchens were in various stages of completion, but work had not commenced on any of the other buildings," reports the Fort Clinch Interpretive Booklet. No heavy guns were placed in the unfinished fort and only a sergeant was designated as caretaker of the fort. On January 7, 1861, a detachment of Florida state militia troops, under the command of Colonel Butler, seized Fort Clinch with no resistance from the caretaker, J.A. Walker, and two laborers.

The Confederates didn't continue to finish the fort's construction due to fears of an immediate attack by Federal gunboats and by marine detachments. Instead, batteries were built within the sand dunes of Amelia and Cumberland Islands. The town of Fernandina and Fort Clinch were surrounded by these batteries as well. State troops were stationed at the fort or nearby. These were the Third, Fourth and Tenth Florida Infantry Regiments, as well as various unattached artillery and cavalry units. Another Florida unit that was stationed at Fort Clinch was the First Florida Battalion, which would later distinguish itself at the battle of Ocean Pond (Olustee). The Twenty-fourth Mississippi Infantry Regiment was the only non-Floridian unit that was stationed at or near the fort.

Early in the war, the Confederate Secretary of State Judah P. Benjamin wrote to Brigadier-General Trapier, who was the commander of the Confederate forces at Fernandina, that the coast of Florida was to be defended at all costs. Therefore, "by the end of February, 1862, thirty guns had been mounted in works about Fernandina—some in Fort Clinch and some behind sand barriers. A few pieces were eight- and ten-inch Columbiads," writes Davis in *The Civil War and Reconstruction in Florida*. General Trapier had stated that the earthworks and trenches that were all over Amelia Island required approximately seven thousand troops; only thirty-five hundred men were actually stationed on the island. The fall of Forts Donelson and Henry in Tennessee proved that troops were needed at the front rather than protecting an indefensible stretch of Florida's coastline.

In February of 1862, General Braxton Bragg, the commander of Confederate forces in East Florida, recommended to the Confederate secretary of state that the Confederacy should abandon Florida and Texas, with the exception of vital ports along the Gulf coasts. The War Department ordered Bragg to abandon East Florida and there were similiar plans for Trapier's forces to abandon Amelia and Cumberland Islands. General Robert E. Lee, the commander of coastal defenses for the states of South Carolina, Georgia and Florida, "suggested that most defense establishments located on islands be evacuated because of the enemy's superior naval forces," reports Johns in *Florida During the Civil War*. The general further felt that Floridian and Confederate troops "should be concentrated in the interior of the state and used to contest an enemy landing after it had taken place rather than to attempt keeping coastal defenses strong enough to repel the initial landing," according to Johns. These recommendations were followed in Florida and were indeed successful when Confederate troops were able to repel Federal forces at the battles of Ocean Pond (Olustee) and of Natural Bridge.

The first unit to depart from Fernandina was the Mississippi Infantry Regiment and further plans were made for an entire evacuation of the island by the remaining troops. With the capture of Confederate ports along the eastern coasts in the north, the port of Fernandina became isolated and its evacuation was hastened. The guns at Fort Clinch were removed by its garrison and the civilian population of Fernandina departed toward the interior of Florida. By March 3, the last train of Confederate troops and supplies, including a few civilians, were departing the island over a trestle bridge when a Union gunboat appeared. The gunboat *Ottawa* began to open fire upon the train. "A solid shot struck the last car, tearing through tables, chairs, and bedsteads, killed two boys seated on a sofa. The wrecked car with its dead was detached and the train, amid the cannon shots of pursuers, went on to safety," writes Davis.

The gunboat was part of a Union invasion force that had set forth from Port Royal at the same time that Confederate forces were evacuating the island and its defenses. The goal of the force was to capture Fort Clinch and Fernandina. The deep harbors of the Cumberland Sound proved to be advantageous to the Federal Navy and the Florida Railroad, which began at the port of Fernandina and led into the interior of Florida, was also mouthwatering to the Federals. The fort, if completed, would protect the harbor entrance and its rear guns were also able to protect the seaport town. Therefore, a company of marines and sailors from the USS *Mohican* seized the strategic fort.

After the seizure of the Amelia and Cumberland Islands, the First New York Volunteer Engineers arrived to complete the construction of Fort Clinch. The engineers' efforts to finish the fort were great and by 1864 the rest of the bastions were finished along with its walls. The infirmary and enlisted men's barracks were also constructed. The enlisted men's barracks were appropriated by the officers for their own use. Though the enlisted men had their officers outnumbered, the remaining space in the barracks was used as a billiard room. The Federal regiments that were stationed or were at Fort Clinch during the War Between the States were the 6th and 7th Connecticut Infantry; 9th and 11th Maine Infantry; 4th New Hampshire Infantry; 157th New York Infantry; 107th Ohio Infantry; 97th Pennsylvania Infantry; 4th South Carolina, black; 1st, 3rd and 34th United States Colored Troops; and 7th United States Infantry.

With Fort Clinch in Union hands, the installation was a staging point for the capture of Jacksonville and the eventual seizure of Florida's interior. The vital Florida town would change hands between Confederate and Union forces at least three times during the war. Many of the units that were stationed at the fort or around Fernandina (such as the Sixth Connecticut Infantry and the Fourth New Hampshire Infantry Regiments) participated in capturing and recapturing the town. On at least one occasion ten of the guns from the fort were used in the bluffs along the St. Johns River during the siege of Jacksonville. But the defeat of the Union forces at Ocean Pond on February 20, 1864, destroyed any plans of Federal control of Florida's interior and reduced these Union forces to staging occasional raids into the interior of the state from Fernandina and Jacksonville.

Fort Clinch and similiar coastal fortifications proved to be obsolete with the siege and fall of Fort Pulaski near Savannah, Georgia. The Georgian fort was one of a string of fortifications that had protected the vital seaport town of Savannah and the entrance to the Savannah River. On April 10–11, 1862, after thirty hours of bombardment from the Union's rifled cannons, the brick fort was knocked into pieces and projectiles were "breaching the casemates and probing for the powder magazine…The white flag went up and the blue-clad artillerists moved in to accept the surrender," writes Foote in *The Civil War, a Narrative: Fort Sumter to Perryville*. The use of rifled cannons was the beginning of the end for the era of brick fortification. However, construction of Fort Clinch had continued to near completion when the installation was deactivated in 1869.

With the war over and Florida back in Union hands, the fort was deactivated and placed under the care of the army's ordnance department from 1869 to 1884. Fort Clinch's arsenal included seventeen cannons that "were in place on permanent mounts when the fort went on caretaker status in April, 1869. Four guns were front pintle 15-inch Rodmans, seven were Model 1844 24-pounder howitzers on flank casemate carriages, the remainder were old model shell guns (1858)," wrote Kemp in his letter. Eventually, the fort was passed on to the Army Corps of Engineers and it wasn't until the Spanish-American War in 1898 that the post was reactivated again.

"An inspection report from two years earlier indicated Fort Clinch was in less than war-readiness condition with the drawbridge planking rotten, sand blocking the entrance, the grounds overgrown, and dismantled guns and building debris scattered about. Drinking water and sanitation facilities were also lacking," describes the Fort Clinch Interpretive Booklet. Many of these old brick forts were reactivated and modified to contain concrete batteries for rifled cannons on disappearing carriages, mortars and/or small rapid firing rifled cannons, due to genuine fear of an attack on the nation's ports from the Royal Spanish Navy.

At Fort Clinch, a poured concrete emplacement for an eight-inch breech-loading rifle was constructed near the north bastion. The gun emplacement used a nearby tunnel as a magazine and a shell hoist was constructed as well. A fire direction and observatory tower was also built and located on the south bastion of the fort. Little documentation exists on whether the gun was actually mounted during that short but "Splendid Little War." "Local oral history says that the gun was transferred in 1903. Unsubstantiated reports say that an old model 8-inch rifle in the Panama Canal Zone in 1937–38 was called the Fort Clinch Gun," writes Kemp. Under the command of Captain J.F. Honeycutt, 209 men from Battery A of the Sixth Coastal Artillery were stationed at the fort during the war and were removed sometime around September 1898.

In 1926, the federal government viewed the fort as being no longer of military use and the site was brought up for sale. At first, the fort was owned by private interests and later the site was purchased by the state. Around 1936, the fort became one of the first state parks in Florida, known as Fort Clinch State Park, and preservation of the fort was carried out by the Civilian Conservation Corps. With the outbreak of the Second World War, Fort Clinch was once more reactivated for military use.

Due to constant harassment of American shipping along the Atlantic coastline of Florida by the German Untersee Boats (U-boats), a surveillance and communication system was installed within the fort by the Coast Guard a few months after the attack on Pearl Harbor on December 7, 1941. "Part of this operation included the Coast Guard's mounted beach patrol who kept watch for landings by saboteurs and spies, among other duties," explains the Fort Clinch Interpretive Booklet. After the war, the fort was returned to the state and it resumed its role as a state park.

In recent years, many of the buildings within the fort have been reconstructed to their 1864 appearance. The storehouse and infirmary are now placed with furniture and equipment of the era, as are the enlisted men's barracks, the prison and the headquarters. Replicas of Rodmans were made in a foundry in Jacksonville and placed about the fort in December of 1968. The only original armaments are the small Model 1844 twenty-four-pounder howitzers that are located in the north bastion of the fort.

A living history program exists at the fort, in which park rangers are dressed in the uniforms of the First New York Engineers and interpret life as it would have been at the post during the War Between the States. A small interpretive center and museum are located near the fort. Today, visitors can visit this sight and view a typical brick seacoast fortification, one of many found along the coasts of the United States, in an excellent state of preservation.

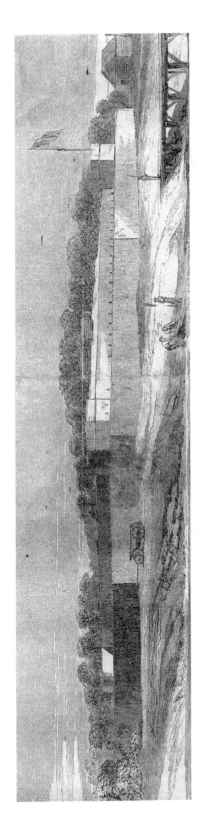

A period illustration showing Fort Clinch as it appeared during the Civil War.

An interior view of the parade ground of Fort Clinch.

Fort Clinch today.

Over the years many of Fort Clinch's buildings were rebuilt and restored to how they appeared during the Civil War.

A twenty-four-pounder howitzer in one of Fort Clinch's bastions.

A living historian depicting a member of the First New York Engineers in the guardhouse of Fort Clinch.

During the Spanish-American War, a poured-concrete emplacement for an eight-inch breech-loading rifle was constructed near the north bastion.

FORT HOUSTON

On March 4, 1865, when news spread of a Union flotilla landing approximately one thousand troops near St. Marks, the citizens of Tallahassee began to build a substantial breastworks on the edge of town where the old Plank Road entered Tallahassee from Newport. It was located on ground that was once part of the plantation of E.A. Houston, father of Captain Patrick Houston (later state adjutant general) who commanded the Confederate artillery at the battle of Natural Bridge. Within the newly built fortification Confederate defenders and citizens of Tallahassee expected to stop the Union advance along the Plank Road to the state capital; however, farther south of Tallahassee both Confederate and Union forces met and fought each other at what would be known as the battle of Natural Bridge. With the roar of battle a few miles distant, Fort Houston did not sustain any attacks by Union forces; however, if the battle had turned against the Confederates, the fort would have been the last position for the Confederates to fall back to and resist the Union thrust into the state capital.

Tallahassee remained the only Confederate state capital east of the Mississippi not to be taken by Union forces during the War Between the States. Today, the square-shaped earthen fortification is about one thousand feet east of the Tallahassee Country Club House and is marked by a row of large live oaks on the circle drive around Duval's Pond. Despite the fact that there are trees within the interior of the fort's battery and in all of its four trenches, the earthen breastworks of Fort Houston are still strongly discernable. A state historical marker now marks "Old Fort Park."

Fort Houston as it appears today.

Located in Tallahassee, Fort Houston's earthworks are preserved in Old Fort Park.

FORT JEFFERSON

The strategic importance of the Tortugas was recognized early. Naval Lieutenant Josiah Tattnall, who surveyed the islands in 1829, pointed out that any nation occupying the Tortugas would control navigation in the Gulf of Mexico. An enemy, seizing the islands, could threaten the growing Mississippi Valley commerce that sailed the Gulf to reach the Atlantic. It was for this reason that the United States War Department decided to fortify the Tortugas and ordered the construction of Fort Jefferson on Garden Key.

Fort Jefferson, with a half-mile perimeter, became the largest link in the chain of seacoast fortifications that the United States undertook to build from Maine to Texas during the first half of the nineteenth century. The walls stood at fifty feet high and eight feet thick. The fort was designed for four hundred fifty guns in three tiers and large enough to garrison fifteen hundred soldiers. Planned and supervised by the United States Corps of Engineers, the fort was started in 1846; but although work continued for almost thirty years, it was never finished. Prior to the outbreak of the War Between the States, most of the labor force consisted of artisans from the North and slaves from Key West. After 1861 the slaves were partly replaced by imprisoned Union deserters, but slave labor didn't end completely until the Emancipation Proclamation went into effect in January 1863.

Federal troops occupied Fort Jefferson throughout the Civil War, but beyond a few shots at passing Confederate blockade-runners, they saw no action. The average garrison numbered five hundred men who spent most of their time building quarters for themselves and their officers. The lack of suitable quarters forced more than one thousand soldiers to build makeshift shelters in wooden sheds and gunrooms. Little important work was done after 1866, for the new rifled cannon introduced during the war had already made the fort obsolete. Moreover, in 1864 engineers conducting subsoil experiments confirmed that the fort's foundation rested not upon a solid coral reef, as had been thought, but upon sand and coral boulders washed up by the sea. The huge structure was settling and the walls began to crack.

During the War Between the States, Fort Jefferson served as a military prison for captured deserters. For almost ten years after the fighting stopped, it remained a prison. Among the prisoners sent there in 1865 were four of the "Lincoln Conspirators"—Michael O'Loughlin, Samual Arnold, Edward Spangler and Doctor Samual Mudd—who had been tried and convicted of complicity in the assassination of President Abraham Lincoln. The most famous of these was Doctor Mudd, a Maryland physician who unknowingly set the broken leg of the assassin John Wilkes Booth. Sentenced to life imprisonment, Mudd was pardoned in 1869 for helping to fight the 1867 yellow fever epidemic that struck the fort, felling 270 out of the 300-man garrison and resulting in 38 fatalities. A historical marker marks the site of Dr. Mudd's cell.

The officers' quarters and enlisted men's barracks were among the first structures begun after the fort was established. The officers' quarters were completed by 1870, but the soldiers' barracks were still unfinished when the army finally abandoned Fort Jefferson in 1874 following a damaging hurricane and another fever outbreak. During the 1880s the American naval fleet used the surrounding waters periodically as an anchorage, and it was from Tortugas Harbor in January 1898 that the battleship *Maine* weighed anchor for Cuba where, one month later, she blew up in Havana Harbor. The army stationed a few troops here during the Spanish-American War, and the navy built a coaling station here in 1898. The fort also contained one of the first naval wireless stations. During the First World War the Tortugas became a seaplane base for a few months. After the war the fort became abandoned. In 1935 President Franklin Delano Roosevelt signed a proclamation naming the fort a national monument and the National Park Service came in to preserve the site for future generations.

Fort Jefferson in the 1880s.

Fort Jefferson as it appeared in a Civil War–period illustration.

Fort Jefferson's enlisted barracks as they appeared in the years following the Civil War. *Courtesy of National Archives.*

The officers' quarters were completed in 1870. *Courtesy of National Archives.*

The parade ground as it appeared during the latter part of the nineteenth century. *Courtesy of National Archives.*

Fort Jefferson's lighthouse and its two tiers of casemates are clearly visible. *Courtesy of National Archives.*

The sally port of Fort Jefferson.

Fort Jefferson is the largest and most isolated of the third system forts. *Courtesy of National Park Service.*

The fort's magazine.

Fort Jefferson's walls have two parallel sides of 325 feet long and the remaining four sides are 477 feet long.

FORT McREE

Named after Lieutenant-Colonel William M. McRee, the fort was at times misspelled in military reports as McRae. Construction began on Fort McRee in 1833 on Foster's Bank at the entrance to Pensacola Harbor and was completed in 1842. The "folded wing" design was shared by Fort Calhoun, later renamed as Fort Wool, in Hampton Roads, Virginia. It was designed to have forty-four seacoast cannons mounted "en casemate" on the two fronts of the fort with twenty-four additional heavy guns on the barbette. The fort was never permanently occupied and was seized by Alabama and Florida state troops, under the command of Lieutenant-Colonel Adam J. Slemmer, on January 21, 1861. The fort was partially destroyed while occupied by Confederate troops during an engagement with Fort Pickens on November 22, 1861. On May 10, 1862, Fort McRee was abandoned by the Confederates. In the decades following the Civil War the fort was destroyed by sweeping tides and pounding surf. The fort's old parade ground is now under the channel of Pensacola Harbor.

Confederate troops in front of Fort McRee.

The interior of Fort McRee as it appeared during the Civil War.

In the years following the Civil War, Fort McRee gradually disappeared as the sea ate away the beach, undermining the fort.

By the twentieth century there was virtually no trace of the fort.

Fort Calhoun (Hampton Roads, Virginia) and Fort McRee (Pensacola, Florida) both shared the "folded wing" design. The partial remains of Fort Calhoun are the only examples of this type of fortification still in existence.

Fort Calhoun's casemates would have been similar to those found within Fort McRee.

EAST AND WEST MARTELLO TOWERS

In 1861 the Federal government began the building of two martello towers, similar to those built during the Napoleonic War, along the shoreline, one near the extreme northeastern end of the island, and the other approximately two miles closer to town. Originally named "Fort Taylor Tower Number One and Advanced Battery" and "Fort Taylor Tower Number Two and Advanced Battery," the towers were meant to supplement Fort Taylor. The military purpose of the two Key West towers was to secure the island and the land side of Fort Taylor by interdicting the fire of vessels covering an amphibious landing. Originally four towers were to be built, but the new rifled ordnance developed during the Civil War superseded their defensive usefulness and only two were built before work was suspended in 1873.

The towers were constructed of brick masonry and reached thirty-six feet in height. They were surrounded by a loopholed counterscarp gallery that had a glacis coupe on its exterior land fronts. On its seaward face the tower had a casemated battery for seacoast guns. Originally the casemated battery was to be of two tiers with eight-inch Columbiads to be emplaced on the second tier and fifteen-inch Rodmans and rifled Parrot guns on the parapet. The tower was to be accessed by a drawbridge connecting the surface of the glacis and the second floor to the tower. Centered on the corners of the top of the towers there were traverse circles for four front-pintle mounted gun carriages. However, the second tier of casemates and the parapet were never completed, nor was any of the armament ever installed.

With the halt of the building, the towers began their decline. Artillerymen from Fort Taylor used West Martello Tower for target practice in the years leading up to the Spanish-American War. In addition, local inhabitants began taking the bricks and other materials for their own uses. In a few years West Martello Tower was in a more ruinous state than its eastern counterpart. On April 26, 1906, a battery for two three-inch model 1903 rapid-fire guns was constructed within the ruined West Martello Tower and named Battery Shadrach Inman. The battery was in service until it was disarmed early in 1946. In 1949 the Key West Art & Historical Society occupied West Martello Tower, later becoming the home for the Joe Allen Garden Center. In 1950 East Martello was also declared surplus. Application for it was made with the blessing of the local naval authorities, for which the upkeep had been problematic. On September 25, 1950, the Art & Historical Society was officially granted permission take possession of the property and turn it into an art gallery and historical museum.

Fort Taylor as seen from the West Martello Tower in Key West in the 1870s.

THE MARTELLO TOWERS ON THE ISLAND OF KEY WEST, FLA.—K41

In the years following the Civil War, gunners from Fort Taylor used the West Martello Tower as target practice. Later Battery Shadrach Inman was constructed in 1904 and was armed with two three-inch rapid-fire guns on M1903 pedestal mounts.

EAST MARTELLO TOWER AND PAN AMERICAN AIRWAYS LANDING FIELD, KEY WEST, FLORIDA

The East Martello Tower as seen from the seashore, 1930s.

Joint military exercise between the Cuban and American soldiers at the East Martello Tower, 1920s. *Courtesy of Key West Art & Historical Society.*

A naval landing party storming the East Martello Tower, 1920s. *Courtesy of Key West Art & Historical Society.*

The East Martello Tower continued serving the military up until World War II. *Courtesy of Key West Art & Historical Society.*

The parade ground of the East Martello Tower.

Today the casemates of the East Martello Tower serve as a historical museum and art gallery.

The Key West Martello Towers were based on the "Tours-Modeles" that were developed in France for coastal defense during the Napoleonic wars.

Seen here is the Napoleonic-era defensive tower of Fort Mississauga in Canada, which clearly shares similarities with the surviving East Martello Tower in Key West.

Another coastal defensive tower in Rochester, England, built in 1812, that displays a few features found in the Key West Martello Towers.

The remains of the West Martello Tower are home for the Joe Allen Garden Center.

Within the West Martello Tower, Battery Shadrach Inman is in an excellent state of preservation.

Fort Pickens

Construction began on the fortification on the western tip of Santa Rosa Island in 1829 and was completed in 1834. The fort, along with Forts Barrancas, McRee and the Advanced Redoubt, was to secure the approaches to Pensacola Bay and the United States Navy Yard. Fort Pickens was pentagonal in shape with a bastion at each of the five corners. The bastions were virtually independent forts themselves, having their own guns and magazine. Covert ways, a dry ditch and flanking outworks completed the fort. Fort Pickens's brick walls were forty feet in height and twelve feet in thickness. Armament consisted of 252 guns of various types and calibers. The peacetime garrison of 100 men could be increased to 1,260 men in time of war.

In the days leading to the outbreak of the War Between the States, Fort Pickens had been unoccupied for several years. The day Florida seceded from the Union on January 10, 1861, the fort became the Federal headquarters for the area. Confederate troops made several attempts to capture Fort Pickens, but all hostilities were stopped when the Confederates evacuated their holdings in the area in May of 1862. The Federals immediately took possession of the other deserted forts and the Navy Yard and held Pensacola for the rest of the war. Toward the end of the war the fort became a military prison. Between 1866 and 1888 the fort served as an internment camp for fifty Chiricahua Apache men, women and children, including the Apache Geronimo and Cochise's son Naiche. The Indians lived in the officers' quarters within the fort.

Toward the end of the nineteenth century new innovations in fortifications and weapons were introduced to Fort Pickens. In 1947 the army declared the fort surplus and it quickly became a state park. Today Fort Pickens is managed by the National Park Service and is part of Gulf Islands National Seashore.

Fort Pickens as it appeared during the Civil War.

In the years following the Civil War, Fort Pickens became a military prison for Apache Indians. *Courtesy of National Archives.*

Each casemate of Fort Pickens contained a gunroom and living quarters, as seen here in this period illustration from *Harper's Weekly*.

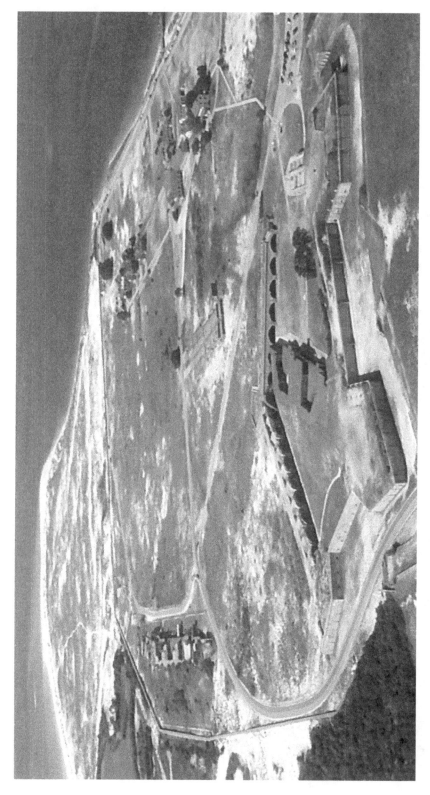

An aerial view showing Fort Pickens and concrete batteries built during the Spanish-American War. *Courtesy of National Park Service.*

A view of one of the bastions as seen through an embrasure.

A Civil War–vintage Rodman cannon on the ramparts of Fort Pickens.

Fort Taylor

Construction of the fort began in 1845 on a shoal off the southwestern shore of the island city of Key West. Because of its strategic location, the fort would have control of all the approaches to the port. In 1850, the fort was named after U.S. President Zachary Taylor, who had died in office earlier that year. The fort was designed by Major General Joseph G. Totten, who later became the first general of the U.S. Army Corps of Engineers. Unlike Fort Jefferson in the Dry Tortugas, which was built at the same time, Fort Taylor was constructed in the form of a trapezoid, the three sides facing seaward, the long side with the main entrance facing land. Connected to land only by a causeway, it was completely surrounded by water. The five-foot-thick walls rose almost fifty feet above sea level with a ground floor and two stories of gunrooms. In addition, there were cisterns for the collection of drinking water below the building. Bricks used in the construction came from Pensacola and Virginia; slate and granite were from Georgia and New England. Irish and German craftsmen did most of the brickwork. The fort contained such unusual features as sanitary facilities flushed by the tide and a desalination plant which produced drinking water from sea water as early as 1861.

In 1854, while the fort was still under construction, 50 cannons and ammunition arrived. The cannons, ten-inch Rodmans, were mounted on the first tier, which was finished by then. By the time the fort was completed, it contained 198 cannons and a large supply of ammunition. The number of troops varied from forty-four in 1861 to five hundred later on. When the War Between the States broke out, the project was still incomplete. Yellow fever, shortages of material and men, remoteness and hurricanes had slowed down progress.

At the outbreak of the Civil War, the action of Captain John Brannan, who occupied Fort Taylor during the night of January 13, 1861, without knowledge of the town's Confederate sympathizers, put the fort in Union hands. Key West was an important outpost of the Union because numerous blockade-running ships were detained at Key West harbor and guarded by Fort Taylor's cannons, a severe loss to the South. Fort Taylor's ten-inch Rodman and Columbiad cannons had a range of three miles. To the Confederate Navy this was an impressive deterrent, preventing any attempt to take the fort and the island of Key West, which remained in Union hands throughout the Civil War. The three-story fort was finally finished in 1866, twenty-one years after it was begun.

In the years that followed, Fort Taylor was again in use during the Spanish-American War. To make way for modern fortifications, the army reduced its height by cutting the fort down to the second-floor level in 1898. This allowed for the installation of newer weapons. Eventually, remodeling also included modifications such as the addition of Battery Adair (four emplacements for 3-inch model 1898 rapid-fire guns on model 1898 masking parapet mounts) and Battery Osceola (emplacements for two 12-inch model 1888 guns on model 1882 barbette carriages) on the inside and filling the gun rooms with obsolete cannons, ordnance, gun carriages and sand to fortify the seaward part of the structure. A number of the old cannons were also embedded in concrete for the same reason. Eight other gun and mortar batteries were built on the land side of Fort Taylor during the turn of the nineteenth and the early years of the twentieth centuries: Battery Covington (two 8-inch model 1888 guns on model 1894 disappearing carriages); Battery John DeKalb (two 6-inch model 1900 guns on model 1900 pedestal mounts), Battery DeLeon (four 10-inch model 1881 M1 and M2 guns on model 1896 disappearing carriages), Battery Dilworth (two emplacements for model 1898 rapid-fire guns on model 1898 masking parapet mounts), Battery Mahlon Ford (two emplacements for 3-inch model 1903 rapid-fire guns on model 1903 pedestal mounts), Battery Gardiner (two 4.7-inch Armstrong quick-firing guns of British manufacture), Battery Shadrach Inman (two 3-inch model 1903 rapid-fire guns on model 1903 pedestal mounts) and Battery Seminole (emplacements for eight 12-inch model 1890 M1 breech-loading mortars on model 1896 M1 mortar carriages).

In the course of the twentieth-century conflicts, more sophisticated weapons and eventually radar and other devices took the place of cannons. Following World War II, in the summer of 1946 the last of the Coast Artillery units stationed in Fort Taylor were deactivated and in the following months the remaining armaments were taken out of service and stored or scrapped. In 1947, the army turned the fort over to the navy. Fort Taylor was designated a national historic landmark in 1973. When the federal government deeded the fort to the State of Florida in 1976, it became a state historic site under the management of the Florida Park Service.

A Civil War view of Fort Taylor, Key West.

Fort Taylor as it appeared in the 1890s. *Courtesy of Florida State Archives.*

The casemates of Fort Taylor. *Courtesy of Florida State Archives.*

A bird's-eye view of Fort Taylor showing the fort's reduction in height and the addition of concrete batteries, 1930s.

U.S. troops storming the beach near Fort Taylor. *Courtesy of Florida State Archives.*

One of Fort Taylor's bastions.

Fort Taylor has one of the largest collections of Civil War–vintage artillery pieces in the country. In recent years many of the artillery pieces were discovered buried in the casemates with sand and debris.

These Rodman cannons were used as fill for the concrete of the Endicott-era batteries in Fort Taylor.

Battery Osceola, Fort Taylor.

The parade ground of Fort Taylor.

Battery Adair, Fort Taylor.

Battery Seminole, Fort Taylor, was once armed with eight twelve-inch 1890 M1 breech-loading mortars.

Battery 231 within the Fort Taylor Reservation was constructed during World War II and was to be armed with six-inch guns with cast steel gun shields.

Fort Walton

Originally called Camp Walton, named after George Walton, a signer of the Declaration of Independence and secretary of East Florida under Andrew Jackson's governorship, this Confederate defense was constructed in 1861 in order to guard East Pass entrance to Santa Rosa. Camp Walton was garrisoned by a company of Florida militia called the "Walton Guards." The militia converted an old Indian mound into an earthwork fortification and mounted a cannon sent from Fort Barrancas by General Braxton Bragg, as well as a naval cannonade that fired eighteen-pound shot. The fort received shelling from Union Field Artillery firing from Santa Rosa Island and several small skirmishes with Federal landing parties occurred near the fort. When the fort was abandoned on August 26, 1861, the cannon was splintered and buried. The fort's garrison later became part of the First Florida Infantry Regiment and served on the Tennessee front in early 1862. The fort's cannon was later unearthed, restored and placed on public display at the base of the Indian mound turned fortification on U.S. 98 in modern-day Fort Walton Beach in Okaloosa County.

Fort Walton and Indian mound that was incorporated as part of the defenses. The spiked cannon was left behind by Confederate troops when they abandoned the fort.

Remains of a large iron basin, used in the evaporating of seawater for salt, came from the Confederate salt works that was destroyed by Union forces during one of their raids into Cedar Key. The large naval cannon in the background is one of two preserved at the Cedar Key State Museum and are the only remnants of the Confederate defenses on Seahorse Key.

A diorama in the Cedar Key State Museum showing Confederate militia defending Fort Number Four against Federal troops during the war. The fort was located on the south side of the railroad bridge (Number Four Bridge) leading to Cedar Key from the mainland.

The oldest building in Cedar Key, made of tabby, was established as a blockhouse during the War Between the States. It is located on the corner of Fourth and G Streets.

YELLOW BLUFF FORT

A Confederate earthen fortification was located on the northern side of the St. Johns River and was one of two major fortifications, with the other located near the modern Ribault Monument on St. Johns Bluff. In November 1861, General Robert Edward Lee, while surveying coast defenses for the Confederacy, recommended that a fortification be placed on the ninety-foot bluff; it is believed that he designed the defenses for Yellow Bluff. By February 1862, General Lee further recommended in a letter to Brigadier General J.H. Trapier that Yellow Bluff be used as the main defense for Jacksonville; however, Union forces attacked the fortifications on St. Johns Bluff and Fort Steele in Mayport, thereby forcing the Confederates to evacuate Yellow Bluff.

Yellow Bluff was later re-occupied by forces under Confederate Captain John Jackson Dickison and, having refortified the defenses, he was able to withstand repeated attacks by Federal gunboats. Union forces regained Yellow Bluff in March 1864 and established a signal station there. The site is located on the New Berlin Road just off State Road 105 (Heckscher Drive).

Yellow Bluff Fort today.

Memorial commemorating the site of Yellow Bluff Fort, located on State Road 105 in Jacksonville.

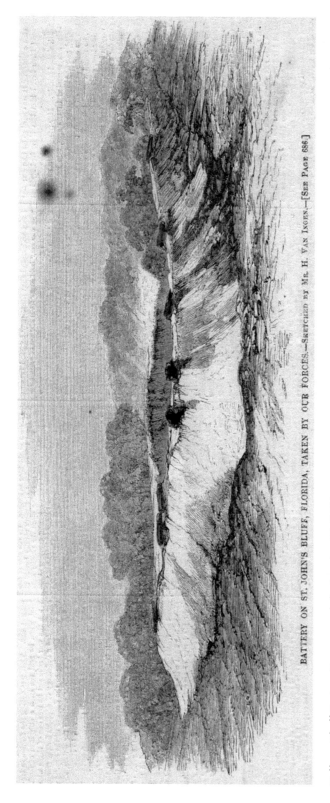

BATTERY ON ST. JOHN'S BLUFF, FLORIDA, TAKEN BY OUR FORCES.—Sketched by Mr. H. Van Ingen.—[See Page 686.]

Yellow Bluff Fort as it appeared during the Civil War.

Natural Bridge Battlefield memorial with traces of Confederate earthworks in the background. This was the site where Confederate troops defeated a large Union force on March 6, 1865, preventing Tallahassee from being captured.

Reconstruction of Confederate defenses within the Natural Bridge Battlefield.

This unknown Confederate fortification once defended the railway bridge over the Suwannee River and is now preserved in the Suwannee River State Park.

Chapter Four
THE MODERN ERA

FORTS DADE AND DESOTO

The official history of the islands of Egmont and Mullet Keys in Tampa Bay began when the schooner *Phoenix* dropped anchor and a group of army engineers rowed ashore on one of the islands in February 1849. These engineers were to survey the Florida coast and make any recommendations on what strategic parts of the state should be fortified for defense. Within this group of army engineer officers was Lieutenant-Colonel Robert Edward Lee. The officers were impressed with the strategic locations of the islands at the mouth of the bay and recommended that the islands be reserved for coastal defense in Florida. A month later, on March 23, Egmont and Mullet Keys were set aside for military purposes by an executive order.

The islands remained unfortified and unmanned for quite a few years with the exception of a temporary stockade in Egmont Key, in which captured Indians were held during the Second and Third Seminole Wars. In 1847, a lighthouse on the northern end of Egmont Key was built to guide ships in and out of Tampa Bay. During the War Between the States, Egmont Key was held by Union forces. A small stockade was erected in order to protect the lighthouse and island from capture by the Confederates. The Union garrison on the island prevented any Confederate blockade-runners from getting through to Tampa with much-needed supplies. On several occasions Federal gunboats and army personnel set out from Egmont Key to attack and bombard Fort Brooke in Tampa. The Confederate forces in Tampa were able to repulse the Federals each time. It wasn't until November 29, 1882, that Egmont and Mullet Keys were finally made into permanent military reservations by another executive order.

On the quiet night of February 15, 1898, an explosion tore apart the United States battleship *Maine* in the harbor of Havana, Cuba; 266 lives were lost with the ship and a war with Spain followed nine weeks later. Many Tampans feared that the Spanish Royal Navy would capture the islands at the mouth of Tampa Bay and from there attack Tampa. Henry B. Plant, a well-known railroad magnate who had placed his tracks across Florida and especially in Tampa, demanded to some of his political friends in Washington that Tampa Bay must be protected. Tampa was also to be the staging point for an American expeditionary force to invade Cuba and Puerto Rico. Congress quickly passed a bill and allotted money for the fortification of Tampa Bay.

Construction hastily began in April of 1898 at Egmont Key and further plans were made to establish a more permanent type of fortification on the two keys. "On July 30, 1898, an allotment of $150,000 was made for a 12-inch mortar battery on Mullet Key. Field work began in November and the work was completed in the Spring of 1900," writes Sarles in his "Historic Sites Report on Fort DeSoto." The battery was to be constructed with emplacements to hold eight mortars and a narrow-gauge railroad was also constructed to bring the huge mortar shells to the battery from the pier. The eastern two-thirds of Mullet Key were transferred by the War Department to the Treasury Department in 1899 for use as a quarantine station. "The rest of Mullet Key became the Fort DeSoto Military Reservation by General Orders No. 43, War Department, of April 4, 1900, which also gave the name of Fort Dade to that on Egmont Key," continues Sarles. Within the same time span of the construction of the mortar battery in Mullet Key, four batteries were built on Egmont Key.

The first battery was constructed on the southern end of Egmont Key and its three gun emplacements were designed to guard the entrance into the south channel. The emplacements held two six-inch Q.F. Armstrong rifles on pedestal mounts and one fifteen-pounder rapid-firing gun on a balanced pillar mount. This is one of the few forts of the era to bear the year of its construction, 1898, upon the steps to its gun emplacements. A command headquarters for the southern battery was constructed under a mound of earth and was located a few hundred feet inland from the battery. Farther up along the beaches of the island, another battery, armed with two eight-inch high-power guns on disappearing carriages, was constructed facing west into the Gulf of Mexico.

The other two batteries were located on the very northern end of the island. One of the batteries was located a few hundred yards from the one facing west and was armed with the same eight-inch high-power guns. The next battery was built on the northern tip of the island, near the lighthouse reservation, and had command of Egmont Channel. It was armed with three fifteen-pounder rapid-firing guns. The post command headquarters, as well as the various warehouses, for both Forts Dade and DeSoto were located nearby. A more sophisticated gauge railroad system was established on Fort Dade and was located throughout the island. The rails began at the pier on the northern tip of the island, where ammunition and supplies would be picked up from military transports and led to the northern, middle and southern batteries. The dozen or so cars were pulled by a steam-driven locomotive and upon one of these cars was mounted a floodlight with a powerful beam of light with a range of several miles.

Both military posts on Egmont and Mullet Keys were placed under the supervision of the post commander at Fort Dade and the forts were treated as a single unit. Forts Dade and DeSoto concentrated their fire in unison when there was any attempt by the enemy to enter the harbor in Tampa Bay. The new fortifications that were being built in Tampa Bay were based on the Endicott System, in which concrete batteries were to replace the old notion of brick fortification.

On Mullet Key, another concrete battery armed with two fifteen-pounder Driggs-Seabury rapid-firing guns was constructed in front of the mortar battery in 1901. Around 1902, the mortars were mounted at Fort DeSoto and the fifteen-pounder guns were installed within the following year. "On May 25, 1903, the mortar battery was named Battery Laidley, and the other, Battery Bigelow," explains Sarles. On both islands barracks and officers' quarters were constructed, with Fort Dade resembling a small town. "In addition to artillery emplacements, roads, houses, a garrison, a jail and a school—some 70 structures in all—were eventually built on the island [of Egmont Key]," writes Hill in "Let It Shine: Modernization will Put Lighthouse on Automatic." The first units to be stationed at the posts were detachments of the First Company, Coast Artillery.

The batteries at Fort DeSoto became an independent post from Fort Dade on February 10, 1904, and remained an independent post until its deactivation in 1910. During a construction project on Fort Dade around April 1907, Fort DeSoto became a temporary headquarters for the Tampa Bay Coastal Artillery. That same month, the First Company was replaced by the Thirty-ninth Company as the new tenants for the forts. In October of 1907, May of 1908 and October of 1909 the new troops were hosts to various elements of the First and Second Infantry of Florida's National Guard in joint exercises on coastal defenses at the two forts. Another local artillery unit, the First Company, Coast Artillery Corps of the National Guard of Florida, participated in these exercises as well.

On June 8, 1910, Fort DeSoto was deactivated as a post and a care-taking detachment, consisting of the 111th and 116th Companies, was sent from Fort Dade to maintain DeSoto's guns and mortars. With America's entry into the First World War, a call was sent out for rapid military mobilization and for heavy guns to be sent to the front. Therefore, "four of DeSoto's eight mortars were shipped away early in 1917, and the protective detachment there was increased during the war," explains Sarles. At the end of the war, on August 31, 1921, Fort Dade was deactivated and the majority of its troops were sent to Key West. A small care-taking detachment was left behind to maintain Forts Dade and DeSoto. It was during this period that the buildings of the two forts began to deteriorate due to a lack of funds.

During 1922, the War Department declared the forts as surplus and both installations were transferred to the quartermaster corps. Forts Dade and DeSoto were officially abandoned on May 25, 1923, and each fort was assigned a civilian caretaker for maintenance. Three years later, Congress authorized the selling of the forts; however, no acceptable bids were received when the two reservations were offered for sale on April 16, 1928. In the following years, further deterioration occurred on the two forts due to a large number of tropical storms. By winter of 1932, the entire structure of Battery Bigelow and nearby barracks on Mullet Key had collapsed into the waters of Tampa Bay. With the closing of the quarantine station on Mullet Key, its land, excluding

Fort DeSoto, was sold to the Pinellas County Board of Commissioners on September 29, 1938. Around the same time, Fort Dade was transferred to the Commerce and Treasury Departments.

As World War II approached, the War Department repurchased Mullet Key and made plans to use it as a bombing range. On March 22, 1941, the island was designated as a sub-post of MacDill Air Field. With the outbreak of the war, Fort Dade was re-commissioned and troops were sent to maintain the installations. There were no major additions on Egmont Key, with the exception of a few concrete pillboxes and various anti-tank traps around the island. After the war, Fort Dade was permanently abandoned in 1946 and Fort DeSoto's use as a bombing range was terminated around June of 1948. Mullet Key and its surrounding islands were purchased by Pinellas County on August 11, 1948. Conditions for the sale stated that the island was to be used as a park and other recreational uses.

On May 11, 1963, Mullet Key was dedicated as the Fort DeSoto Park and became part of Pinellas County's park system. The mortar battery, Battery Laidley, is now preserved intact with its four remaining twelve-inch mortars. However, the battery for the two fifteen-pounder rapid-firing guns, Battery Bigelow, couldn't be saved from the many tropical storms of Florida and from ongoing beach erosion. Its remains can still be detected not too far away from the recreational pier. Fort DeSoto's batteries joined the National Register of Historical Places on June 22, 1977. Nearby, the fortified island of Egmont Key is crumbling to oblivion due to neglect, beach erosion and vandalism.

The island was declared a Wild Life Refuge in 1974 and was named to the National Register of Historic Places in January of 1979. But, the agency responsible for the care of Egmont Key, U.S. Fish and Wildlife, was usually undermanned and under-budgeted to carry out any effective preservation of the island and of the remains of Fort Dade. The island became a popular picnic and beach area for weekend boaters. "Some of those visitors dump beer cans and other rubbish on the 300-acre island. Others shoot bullet holes through $350 refuge warning signs, set fires and streak graffiti through the crumbling, concrete military village that is a relic of the Spanish-American War," writes Wares in her essay "Tampa Bay Wildlife Refuges: Inhabitants Compete with Man for Survival." Occasionally, the Coast Guardsmen from the lighthouse reservation would help out the U.S. Fish and Wildlife agents by confiscating relics found at the fort by visitors.

Next to vandals and negligent visitors, Mother Nature has taken the greatest toll upon the island. Due to the many tropical storms that wreaked havoc on the island in the 1980s, the southern battery that once held the two Armstrong rifles is now under the waters of the Gulf of Mexico. Portions of the ammo dump are gone as well, with the middle batteries being next in line for destruction. Also, natural sediment erosion undermined many of the buildings and other structures. In recent years, efforts have been made to preserve what's left of the island and of the fort. The two six-inch Q.F. Armstrong rifles and their mounts were removed from the remains of the south battery on April 12–14, 1980, and were restored by the Pinellas County Park Department. After two years of research and restoration, the guns were placed in the Fort DeSoto Park as a permanent memorial to Fort Dade. The four remaining mortars, model 1890 (manufactured by Watervliet Arsenal in 1902), are the only ones existing in the continental United States.

As a final footnote, two of the Fort Dade Guns (eight-inch model 1888 M2 on disappearing carriage model 1896) were removed from Battery McIntosh at Fort Dade (Egmont Key) and placed as a war memorial at the old Tampa Bay Hotel, site of General Shafter's headquarters during the Spanish-American War, by the United Spanish War Veterans on November 7, 1927, while the other gun of the same type and from the same battery was also set up next to the old American Legion Building in St. Petersburg. During World War II both the guns and carriages from Tampa and St. Petersburg were scrapped. After the war another gun (eight-inch model 1888 M1) on a World War I railway carriage (M1918) was placed on the monument's base in the University of Tampa's grounds. The gun barrel itself originally came from Fort Morgan, Alabama, and was originally on a disappearing carriage of the same model as the ones used at Fort Dade. In 1944, this gun was reported stationed at Camp Eustis, Virginia, and after the war someone realized that this gun was of the same or at least similar design as the original Fort Dade gun that was scrapped during the war and acquired it for a newly restored memorial. There are no components of the original Fort Dade gun to be found on the gun of the present memorial.

Six-inch disappearing gun on Battery Guy Howard, Fort Dade on Egmont Key. *Courtesy of Pinellas County Historical Commission.*

Inspection in front of the enlisted barracks, Fort DeSoto, circa 1905. Courtesy of Pinellas County Historical Commission.

Sergeant H. Hewas was in charge of Fort Dade's post power plant, 1914–21. Courtesy of Pinellas County Historical Commission.

Coast Artillerymen ramming home a projectile into the breech of a twelve-inch model 1890 mortar, Battery Laidley, Fort DeSoto.

Fort DeSoto's four remaining mortars are the only ones left in the continental United States. A young author in the Spanish-American War–era uniform of the 1st United States Artillery at the time when he began a living history program at the fort in the early 1990s. *Courtesy of Pinellas County Historical Commission.*

Soldiers loading a practice buoy at the end of the Engineer's Wharf, Fort Dade. A tug would pull the buoy for artillery practice. *Courtesy of Pinellas County Historical Commission.*

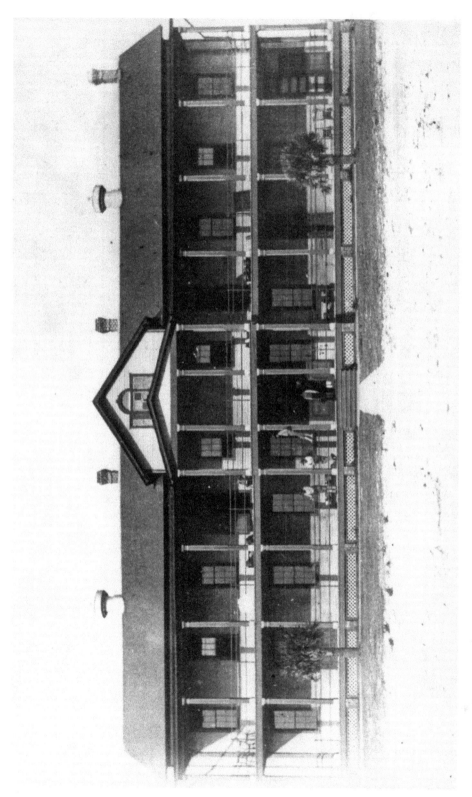

Enlisted barracks, Fort DeSoto, 1905. *Courtesy of Pinellas County Historical Commission.*

Soldiers with a pelican and a shark on Engineer's Wharf on the north side of Egmont Key, 1902. *Courtesy of Pinellas County Historical Commission.*

A six-inch model 1898 Armstrong gun of Battery Burchsted, Fort Dade, 1902. *Courtesy of Pinellas County Historical Commission.*

The eight-inch disappearing guns from Battery McIntosh, Fort Dade, were donated to the State of Florida on June 11, 1923. One went to Plant Park in Tampa as a Spanish-American War memorial (seen here), while the other went to the American Legion building in St. Petersburg. Both were scrapped during World War II. *Courtesy of Tampa-Hillsborough County Public Library System.*

One of two six-inch model 1898 Armstrong guns rescued from Battery Burchsted, Fort Dade in 1980 and now preserved in front of Battery Laidley, Fort DeSoto.

The scrapped Tampa gun was replaced with an eight-inch M1918 gun on railway mount that was originally from Fort Morgan, Alabama.

Battery Charles Mellon, Fort Dade, as it appears today.

PENSACOLA'S CONCRETE BATTERIES

With the end of the Civil War, seacoast fortifications of the second and third systems, such as Forts Pickens, McRee and Barrancas, became obsolete with the introduction of the rifled cannon. By the 1870s new advances were made with ironclad warships armed with powerful breech-loading rifled cannons. Therefore, a new system of fortifications was needed and it wasn't until 1885 that a board was organized by Secretary of War William C. Endicott to study and propose a plan. This would mark the beginning of the Endicott system of fortifications, remnants of which can be found today in Pensacola Bay and in the rest of coastal America.

Between 1887 and 1896, twenty-three harbors, including Pensacola Bay, were designated for modern fortifications with more to be assigned in the following years. Defense objectives for Pensacola were still the same as they were in previous years: to protect the naval base and port from enemy attack. In 1893 a board of engineers was sent to examine potential sites in the Pensacola Bay area. "Upon reconnoitering Santa Rosa Island, the Board found that Fort Pickens, which had served the Union well during the Civil War, was in fair condition" and that the parade ground "was roomy, affording a good position for a lift battery, while many good positions were available for rapid-fire guns to protect the submarine minefield," writes Bearss in his "Historic Structure Report and Resource Study." Fort McRee, on Perdido Key, "was in ruins, most of the fabric having been undermined by the sea and distributed along the shore by waves. The narrow bank was protected by two concrete groins and the rubble of the 1830s fort," continues Bearss.

The final decisions of the board called for a disappearing battery with two ten-inch guns on the former site of Fort McRee, a lift battery with two twelve-inch guns on the parade grounds of Fort Pickens and both disappearing and mortar batteries to be established on Santa Rosa Island. The old Fort Barrancas was to retain its Civil War–period converted eight-inch rifled Rodmans for protection of the beaches and of the area within the bay. Another form of protection was the submarine mine defenses, in which "the mines and their miles of control cable were stored ashore so they could be planted rapidly in the event of war," reports "Concrete Batteries—The Endicott System." A new branch within the army was formed and designated as the Coast Artillery. Construction would soon begin on Santa Rosa Island.

The first structure to be constructed was located west of Fort Pickens and therefore protected the harbor entrance and defended the island from amphibious attack. The structure used to be a single battery but it was separated into two separate batteries in 1916. These structures were known as Battery Cullum and Battery Sevier. When the batteries were completed in 1898, they were armed with four ten-inch rifled cannons on disappearing carriages. Both batteries were equipped with their own fire control equipment and electric plant. The magazines were lined with bricks and ceiled with lead in order to prevent water and moisture leakage onto the ammunition. In later years, the magazines were layered in copper. The batteries were to be manned by soldiers of the Thirteenth Coast Artillery.

Immediately after the First World War, the batteries were declared surplus and two of the guns from Battery Cullum were dismounted and shipped away. The War Department reverted its earlier decision and replaced Battery Cullum with two new model 1895 ten-inch guns in 1921. During 1922–23, Batteries Cullum and Sevier were equipped with a new power station built within a reinforced concrete structure. In the 1930s, the War Department realized that some of their coastal fortifications were becoming obsolete. An order was sent to the Fort Pickens installation and "upon receipt of this order, dated June 16, 1933, the four 10-inch guns had their breech mechanisms removed and were given a heavy coat of cosmoline," describes Bearss. The batteries' guns were later removed and scrapped around November 1942.

In 1943, with World War II already in progress, Batteries Cullum and Sevier were armed with 3-inch rapid-fire guns. Also battery commander, coincidence range finder, signal and meteorological stations were constructed on or near the old batteries. The adjacent Battery Van Swearingen, quickly built in 1898 and armed with two 4.7-inch Armstrong rapid-fire guns due to fears of a Spanish naval attack during the Spanish-American War, was armed with 3-inch rapid-fire guns and a range finder station. In June 1946, approximately a year after the end of the Second World War, the 3-inch guns on Batteries Cullum, Sevier and Van Swearingen were dismounted and scrapped.

Batteries Pensacola and Worth were constructed in 1899, a year after Battery Van Swearingen. Battery Pensacola was constructed on the parade grounds of Fort Pickens and was armed with two twelve-inch rifled guns on disappearing carriages. One of Fort Pickens's bastions was totally destroyed when a fire ignited the ammunition that was stored in the area on June 20, 1899. The powerful recoil of the battery's twelve-inch guns had weakened some sections of the old masonry fort during the few short years of the battery's existence. Some portions of Fort Pickens's walls were reduced in order for the observers to fully direct the line of fire from the battery's guns. In the summer of 1933, the War Department declared the battery surplus and the following year its guns were removed. During the Second World War, the guns' carriages were scrapped and the battery served as a storage facility for the Coast Artillery.

Battery Worth was constructed to hold eight twelve-inch mortars, with an observation station in between the two mortar pits. However, after the First World War the military removed four of the already obsolete mortars. The remaining four mortars continued in active service until May 1942, when they were finally removed and scrapped. "During the 1930s, the four 12-inch mortars of Battery Worth, along with the 12-inch rifles of Battery Langdon, constituted Tactical Fire Group No. 2," writes Bearss. After the battery had the last of its mortars removed, it continued to serve the Coast Artillery during the Second World War. The old bombproofs and magazines were converted to hold a harbor defense command post and a harbor entrance control post as well as a fire control switchboard room. At the same time that Batteries Pensacola and Worth were being built, another site of a Civil War fort was being installed with similar coastal batteries nearby.

West of the ruins of Fort McRee on Perdido Key, a battery armed with two eight-inch breech-loading guns on disappearing carriages was constructed in 1899. The coastal fortification was to be named Battery Slemmer, after the Civil War Union officer who denied the Confederates in apprehending Fort Pickens. The battery and later fortifications were to form a military installation under the revived name of Fort McRee. A year after the installation of Battery Slemmer, another was constructed on the left flank of the battery. This was Battery Center and was armed with four fifteen-pounder Driggs-Seabury rapid-fire guns. Both installations were declared obsolete after the end of the First World War and their guns were dismounted by 1920.

In 1904 and 1905, two more batteries were added to the Fort Pickens area on the western end of Santa Rosa Island north of the harbor entrance. These were Batteries Payne and Trueman. The design and function of the batteries were identical: to defend the submarine minefield and the channel from enemy minesweepers and torpedo boats. Each battery was armed with two three-inch model 1902 rapid-fire guns, thus enabling the batteries to provide 360-degree fire. "In the early 1920s, the three extant rapid-fire batteries [Payne, Trueman and Center] were programmed to receive coincidence range-finder stations," reports Bearss. Due to threats of German U-boats in the Gulf of Mexico during the Second World War, the two guns from Battery Trueman were relocated to Battery Cullum in 1943. During the summer of 1946 the obsolete guns from Batteries Payne and Trueman were dismounted and salvaged.

Battery Cooper, armed with two six-inch model 1903 guns on disappearing carriages, was constructed south of Battery Worth in 1905. In November 1917, due to America's entry into the First World War, the battery's guns were shipped to France for use as railway guns. The carriages were later removed in 1920. During the late 1930s four 155mm model 1918 General Purpose Firing (GPF) guns were installed in front of Battery Cooper as part of the Harbor Defense Project. The battery's guns were removed in April 1945 and the installation was abandoned. In 1976 the National Park Service and the Smithsonian Institute installed a gun that was identical to the one that was originally located on Battery Cooper.

Within ten years after the construction of Battery Cooper, the War Department believed that a number of concrete fortifications were becoming obsolete by the eve of America's entry into World War I. Therefore, a more advanced fortification was constructed about two miles east of Fort Pickens, commencing in 1917. The battery was to be armed with two twelve-inch guns en barbette. There was a lack of manpower in constructing the battery due to the war in Europe, and it wasn't until 1923 that the new battery was finally finished. The new coastal fortification was named Battery Langdon, in honor of a Civil War officer who was stationed at Fort Pickens and saw combat in the battle of Olustee during the War Between the States. A gauge railroad was constructed between Battery Worth and Battery Langdon for transportation of supplies and ammunition to the batteries in the area.

With the surprise attack on Pearl Harbor, the United States was thrust into a new war in which radical changes would have to be made in tactics and in fortifications. Bearss writes that between September 1, 1939, and December 7, 1941, the American military had learned from the war in Europe that

> *devastating attacks by "Stuka" dive bombers had been particularly demoralizing to artillerists manning guns where there was no overhead protection. In the Philippines those coastal defense guns and mortars of Corregidor and the other Manila Bay forts mounted "en barbette" or pits, without overhead cover, were either disabled or neutralized by aerial bombardment and the fire of Japanese heavy artillery in April and early May 1942.*

Learning from these facts, heavy casemates of reinforced concrete were constructed over Battery Langdon during 1942–43. The gun crews were now protected with seventeen feet of masonry placed overhead and walls ten feet thick. With the addition of these casemates, the guns' effectiveness was reduced from a 360-degree radius to 145 degrees. Even the magazines were reinforced with heavy concrete and the entire battery was covered in twenty feet of sand fill. Next to giving older batteries a new facelift, a newer type of battery was to be adopted by the Coast Artillery.

The new batteries' six-inch guns were not required to be casemated as Battery Langdon's were; instead they "were to be provided with all round curved shields of cast-steel four to six inches thick. These shields, which resembled turrets, furnished protection against machine gun and light artillery fire," writes Bearss. A single battery was armed with two six-inch shield guns and in between these two guns an earth-covered concrete traverse was built. This earthen mound contained a magazine, a communication room, a storage facility, a power station and space for air conditioning equipment. These fortifications were designated as Batteries Number 233 and Number 234. Battery Number 233 was located on the former site of Fort McRee, next to Batteries Slemmer and Center, on Perdido Key, and Battery Number 234 was located several hundred yards west of Battery GPF, formerly Battery Cooper.

Construction was completed in the autumn of 1943 for Batteries Number 233 and Number 234. Near Number 234, a tower was constructed in order to direct the battery's guns. By then the course of the war in Europe and in the Pacific was going against the Germans, Italian and Japanese military powers. The new fortifications were given low priority and it wasn't until 1946, approximately a year after the end of the Second World War, that the batteries' shields and gun carriages were received by the Pensacola Harbor Defense Command. Batteries Number 233 and Number 234 never received their six-inch guns; the new batteries were declared obsolete after the end of the war. In 1976, the National Park Service and the Smithsonian Institution installed two six-inch shielded guns on Battery Number 234 in order to show park visitors how the battery would have looked if the guns had been emplaced by the soldiers of the Thirteenth Coast Artillery.

The end of the Second World War brought seacoast fortifications into obsolescence. D-Day proved that the mighty Nazi coastal fortifications were of no use under heavy naval bombardment and massive amphibious assaults. During the summer of 1947, the army decided to deactivate Forts McRee and Pickens. All remaining guns, carriages and shields from the various batteries were removed and scrapped. Following the deactivation of Forts McRee and Pickens, the Coast Artillery Corps was disbanded as well.

For many years the sites remained neglected. On January 8, 1971, Congress enacted Public Law 91-660 declaring the establishment of the Gulf Islands National Seashore. The new law required that Forts McRee and Pickens, with other colonial and Civil War–era fortifications in the Pensacola area, would be maintained by the National Park Service. After major renovations, the National Park Service opened Fort Pickens and its batteries on Santa Rosa Island in 1976. The batteries of Fort McRee remain isolated, a two- to three-hour hike from Johnson Beach on Perdido Key.

The preserved concrete batteries of the Pensacola Bay area show America's final attempt in protecting its shores with big guns and massive forts. However, these fortifications proved to be obsolete in the face of continuing advancements in military technology, such as combined air and sea attacks. Today, these batteries show the many structural styles that were used between 1890 and 1947. These batteries serve as a reminder to present and future park visitors of a bygone era in America's desire for self-defense.

Battery Pensacola as it appears today.

A twelve-inch disappearing gun firing during a training exercise at Battery Pensacola, Fort Pickens, 1900. *Courtesy of Gulf Islands National Seashore, National Park Service.*

A ten-inch disappearing gun at Battery Cullum-Sevier, which was constructed in 1898 as two separate structures. *Courtesy of Gulf Islands National Seashore, National Park Service.*

Battery Cullum-Sevier.

Battery Langdon.

One of two twelve-inch guns "en barbette" being cut for scrap during the closing days of World War II. Battery Langdon. *Courtesy of Gulf Islands National Seashore, National Park Service.*

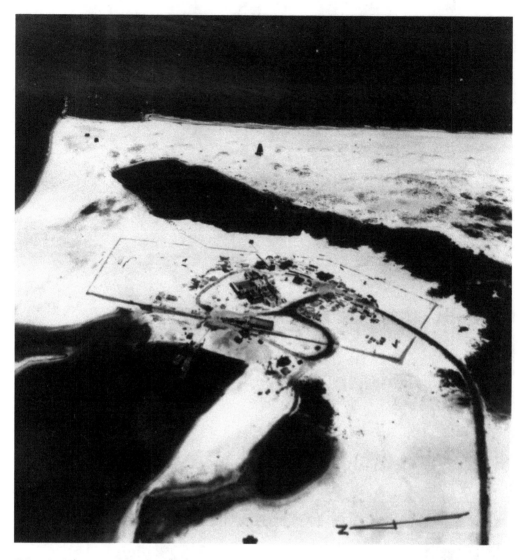

Batteries Slemmer (1899) and Center (1900) on Perdido Key formed the military installation under the revived name of Fort McRee. *Courtesy of Gulf Islands National Seashore, National Park Service.*

Completed in 1899, Battery Worth housed eight twelve-inch mortars in two gun pits. *Courtesy of Gulf Islands National Seashore, National Park Service.*

The battery lost half of its armaments in 1918; however, it continued service until 1942. This was how the battery appeared in 1996. *Courtesy of Gulf Islands National Seashore, National Park Service.*

The plotting room for Battery Worth in Fort Pickens during the early days of World War II. *Courtesy of Gulf Islands National Seashore, National Park Service.*

Soldiers posing with a submarine mine in the Fort Pickens Military Reservation, 1907. *Courtesy of Gulf Islands National Seashore, National Park Service.*

These soldiers are posing with a 4.72-inch Armstrong rifle in Battery van Swearingen, Fort Pickens. *Courtesy of Gulf Islands National Seashore, National Park Service.*

Battery 234 was one of the last of the modern concrete batteries completed in Fort Pickens in 1943; it was never activated. *Courtesy of Gulf Islands National Seashore, National Park Service.*

A lonely fire control station on the western end of Santa Rosa Island between Batteries Trueman and Payne.

A six-inch gun, originally from West Point, in Battery Cooper. In the distance is the fire control tower of Battery 234. *Courtesy of Gulf Islands National Seashore, National Park Service.*

PASS-A-GRILLE POINT

World War II brought new life into the St. Petersburg area, a city that had suffered heavily with the bust of land speculation in the 1920s and a declining tourist industry. After the Japanese attack on Pearl Harbor and the United States' declaration of war, the Tampa Bay area was "invaded" by thousands of military personnel of all branches of the military. As if overnight, every hotel and apartment building in St. Petersburg was taken by the military for use as barracks for its men. The Don Cesar building was purchased by the army for use as a military hospital. (During the war years the Don Cesar would be known as Flak Hotel.) The army then moved downward into Pass-A-Grille, a sleepy little community south of the Don Cesar.

On October 20, 1942, elements of the Fifty-third Coast Artillery took possession of the southern tip of the island from Third Avenue down to the tip where Pass-A-Grille Pass leads into the intercoastal waterways of the Gulf Beaches and Tampa Bay. The army relocated most of the residents out of the newly designated military installation with the exception of Mrs. Thomas Watson, the eighty-five-year-old widow of the co-inventor of the telephone. The top brass decided to string barbed wire around the house, making it a civilian enclave bordered on three sides by a military installation.

Four 155mm mobile seacoast guns and anti-aircraft guns soon took their place from sandbagged emplacements. Two observation towers along with hutments and tents for the gun crews were the first defensive measures taken at the point. Construction soon began on permanent gun emplacements, barracks, a theater, administrative and storage buildings. A post exchange was also established at the new base. Many of the homes that fell within the military installation were utilized by the Fifty-third CA for various purposes, such as Mr. Crawley's old house that became battery headquarters for the Coast Artillery unit.

Many of the men from the base spent their leisure time in nearby St. Petersburg. Residents recalled seeing servicemen marching up and down on Central Avenue and lining up for meals in hotels and theatres that had been converted to barracks and mess halls. As the Allies were making advances on all the fronts of the European and Pacific theaters, many units meant for harbor defense at home were transferred to more vital areas in the war effort. During the spring of 1944 the 53rd was replaced by Battery F, 31st Coast Artillery (re-designated as the 252nd Coast Artillery). By the end of November 1944, the Coast Artillery pulled out from the point. However, the installation was quickly absorbed by the Army Air Force Convalescent Hospital, located in the former Don Cesar Hotel, on December 30, 1944. The vacated barracks and homes at Pass-A-Grille Point were used by the hospital's clerks, medics, drivers, cooks and technicians. A detachment of military police encamped on the nearby beach.

With the capitulation of Nazi Germany, the Army Air Force Convalescent Hospital, including the former Coast Artillery installation at the point, was deactivated on June 30, 1945. A few of the buildings built by the army CA still stand in Pass-A-Grille Point, though they are presently indistinguishable in their civilian dress. One wooden structure believed to be one of the barracks on the southern half of Third Avenue is currently used as an apartment; another structure believed to be one of the administrative buildings is on the corner of First Avenue and Pass-A-Grille Way. Next to the remaining buildings one can still see the partially buried concrete obstacles on the beach. These reminders reflect upon a time when we prepared for a war on the homefront as well as the frontlines.

Members of Battery B, Fifty-third Coast Artillery, who were stationed in Pass-a-Grille during World War II. *Courtesy of Pinellas County Historical Commission.*

The Spanish-American War–era battery on St. Johns Bluff. *Courtesy of Florida State Archives.*

ST. JOHNS BLUFF BATTERY

This was a concrete battery that protected the entrance to the St. Johns River with its two eight-inch breech-loading rifles. A railroad tram was constructed to bring construction material and, later, ammunition up to the concrete battery. The fortification was in active military use for less than a year and a half, from April 1898 to October 1899; for that reason alone the installation was never properly named or given a battery number. It is usually referred to by the locals as the Jacksonville fort. The battery was dismantled in October 1899 and the guns sent to Fort Pickens in Pensacola. Located off Fort Caroline Road, the emplacements are near the site of Fort Caroline National Park. The old concrete battery can still be seen today and is in relatively good condition.

As fixed defenses and fortifications became obsolete after the First and Second World Wars, new means in defending Florida and the United States were built, but they can be used for offensive means as well. An example is this abandoned Cold War–era U.S. Army HAWK missile battery located by the Key West International Airport. These military installations were typical of the defenses built throughout south Florida during the Cold War (1946–1991).

Fort Brickell

After the destruction of the U.S. battleship Maine on February 18, 1898, and the subsequent road to war with Spain, many Miamians feared a Spanish attack in spite of the shallow channel. In response the United States government erected a temporary battery on Brickell property, one and a half miles south of Brickell Point and five hundred feet east of the historical marker located on Brickell Avenue, Miami. The "fort," which commanded the channel, consisted of an earth mound covering the magazine, two guns and a one-hundred-foot semicircular parapet. The Spanish-American War ended on August 12, 1898, and by September the guns had been removed from Fort Brickell.

During the 1950s and up to the Cuban Missile Crisis, fallout shelters and bunkers began appearing in public buildings and even in people's backyards. This Cold War relic was found on the corner of MacDill Avenue and West Cleveland Street in Tampa. It was destroyed during the winter (October–November) of 2011 in order to enlarge a parking lot for an office building.

Cold War Defenses

Despite the undetected arrival of a defecting Cuban B-26 Invader at Daytona Beach Airport in January 1959, the vulnerability of America's southern frontier was not apparent until the Cuban Missile Crisis. As part of the nation's posturing against the Soviet Union over the issue of missiles in Cuba, a rapid buildup of forces occurred in Florida. Part of this buildup included antiaircraft missile batteries. Command of the arriving missile units was assumed by the Headquarters and Headquarters Battery, 13th Artillery Group, formerly of Fort Meade, Maryland, which arrived at Homestead AFB on October 30, 1962. By November 8, this command unit had moved four miles north to a location at Princeton. Initially deploying MIM-23 HAWK mobile batteries, once it became evident that the missile deployment would be long-term, the batteries were repositioned and permanent structures were built that employed above-ground Nike-Hercules missiles. Missile batteries in southern Florida continued on active duty until 1979, well beyond the 1975 demise of ARADCOM.

Army Air Defense Command Post (AADCP) HM-01DC was established at Richmond AFS, Florida, in 1961 for Nike missile command-and-control functions. The site was equipped with the AN/GSG-5(V) BIRDIE solid-state computer system. In 1965, it was upgraded to the AN/FSG-1 Missile-Master Radar Direction Center. One height-finder radar was later removed, and the remaining set was modified to an AN/FPS-116 c. 1977. HM-01DC was integrated with the USAF Air Defense Command/NORAD Semi Automatic Ground Environment (SAGE) air defense radar network as Site Z-210. The site was demolished by Hurricane Andrew on August 24, 1992, and subsequently closed.

The following sites were built in South Florida: HM-01 HM-03 Opa Locka/Carol City; HM-01DC HM-01DC Richmond AFS; HM-40 Key Largo; HM-65, redesignated HM-66, Florida City; HM-69 Florida City, in Everglades NP; HM-85 10 southwest Miami; HM-95 southwest Miami; HM-97 West Homestead; HM-99 West Homestead. Of these, HM-69 has been preserved by the National Park Service and is open for tours during the winter months.

In addition, there were HAWK missile sites scattered throughout Florida that served as the air defense for strategic bases and large centers of population. Of these is the U.S. Army–built HAWK missile site in Key West, Florida, as a link in the defensive perimeter; it was constructed during the Cold War. The antiaircraft facility, unusual because it was built as a permanent installation, was intended to guard against attack from Cuba, ninety miles away. In 1979, it closed, and although the property continues to be maintained by the Naval Air Station, Boca Chica Field, to date no new use has been found for the facility. It sits abandoned, collecting rust and graffiti.

Today, reminders of the Cold War in Florida are fast disappearing. Fallout shelters are few and far between as remaining examples are razed to make way for modern developments. One fallout shelter of note has been preserved. President John F. Kennedy, who was facing a possible "hot war" with the Soviets, recommended a fallout shelter for all Americans "as rapidly as possible" in an October 1961 speech. Two months later, Kennedy was presented with his own top-secret tropical bomb shelter off Palm Beach, Florida, on an inlet of the Atlantic Ocean. Termed the "Detachment Hotel" in documents, the fallout shelter there was built by Navy Seabees in less than two weeks at the end of December 1961 and sits a short stroll from a rambling Colonial-style house that doubled as a United States Coast Guard station. Deftly camouflaged by trees, it was hard to spot. In those days, if people asked, they would be told it was a munitions depot—nothing more. Kennedy visited the bunker twice during a drill. The government never declared its existence until 1974. Today, it is part of the Palm Beach Maritime Museum, a nonprofit organization that leases part of the land on Peanut Island and runs tours of the bunker and the former Coast Guard station. But according to local residents, the bunker "was the worst-kept secret in Palm Beach."

Bibliography

Bearss, Edwin C. Historic Structure Report and Resource Study, Pensacola Harbor Defense Project, 1890–1947. Florida Unit, Gulf Islands National Seashore, Escambia and Santa Rosa Counties, Florida, March 1982 (document obtained through Denver Technical Information Center, D-1878).

Bennett, Charles E. *Florida's "French" Revolution, 1793–1795*. Gainesville: University Presses of Florida, 1981.

———. "Fort Caroline, Cradle of American Freedom." *Florida Historical Quarterly* XXXV, no.1 (July 1956).

Boone, Floyd E. *Boone's Florida Historical Markers and Sites*. Moore Haven, FL: Rainbow Books, 1988.

Boyd, Mark F. "Events at Prospect Bluff on the Apalachicola River, 1808–1818." *Florida Historical Quarterly* XVI, no.2 (October 1937).

———. "The Federal Campaign of 1864 in East Florida." *Florida Historical Quarterly* XXIX, no.1 (July 1950).

———. "The Fortifications at San Marcos de Apalache." *Florida Historical Quarterly* XV, no.1 (July 1936).

———. "The Joint Operations of the Federal Army and Navy near St. Marks, March 1865." *Florida Historical Quarterly* XXIX, no.2 (October 1950).

Burns, Zed H. *Confederate Forts*. Natchez, MS: Southern History Publications, Inc., 1977.

Chatelain, Verne E. *The Defenses of Spanish Florida, 1565 to 1763*. Washington, D.C.: Carnegie Institution of Washington, 1941.

Coleman, James C. and Irene S. *Guardians on the Gulf: Pensacola Fortifications, 1698–1980*. Pensacola: Pensacola Historical Society, 1982.

Coles, David J. "'Hell-By-The-Sea': Florida's Camp Gordon Johnston in World War Two." *Florida Historical Quarterly* LXXIII, no. 1 (July 1994): 1–22.

"Concrete Batteries and Coast Artillery." Pamphlet-booklet printed by Eastern National Park and Monument Association for use by Gulf Islands National Seashore, ca. 1980.

"Concrete Batteries—The Endicott System." *Barnacle* (summer 1983): 6.

Covington, James W. "An Episode in the Third Seminole War." *Florida Historical Quarterly* XLV, no. 1 (July 1966).

———. "Life at Fort Brooke". *Florida Historical Quarterly* XXXVI, no. 4 (April 1958): 319-330.

Cragg, Dan. *Guide to Military Installations*. Harrisburg, PA: Stackpole Books, 1991.

Davis, T. Frederick. "Fort Caroline." *Florida Historical Quarterly* XII, no. 2 (October 1933).

Davis, William Watson. *The Civil War and Reconstruction in Florida*. New York: Columbia University Press, 1913.

Deagan, Kathleen, and Darcie MacMahon. *Fort Mose: Colonial America's Black Fortress of Freedom*. Gainesville: University Press of Florida, 1995.

de Quesada, Alejandro M. *Distant Thunder: The United States Artillery from the Spanish-American War to the Present*. London: Greenhill Books, 2001.

———. "Guarding the Skies Over Pass-A-Grille." *The Veterans Sentinel* (February 1994): 6.

———. *The Men of Fort Foster*. Union City, TN: Pioneer Press, 1996.

———. *The Spanish-American War in Tampa Bay*. Charleston, SC: Arcadia Publishing, 1998.

———. *World War Two in Tampa Bay*. Charleston, SC: Arcadia Publishing, 1997.

Dowdey, Clifford, and Louis H. Manarin, eds. *The Wartime Papers of Robert E. Lee*. New York: Da Capo Press, 1987.

Dunn, Hampton. "Then & Now: Ft. Homer Hesterly." *St. Petersburg Times*, November 10 1993, community times section.

Duren, Lieutenant C.M. "The Occupation of Jacksonville, 1864, and the Battle of Olustee." *Florida Historical Quarterly* XXXII, no.4 (April 1954).

Eden, John H. *Fort Cooper—April 1836*. Inverness, FL: R.G. Printing Co., 1977.

Fitzgerald, Edmund, and James R. Hinds. *Bulwark and Bastion*. Las Vegas: Council on Abandoned Military Post Periodical, 1981.

Foote, Shelby. *The Civil War, a Narrative: Fort Sumter to Perryville*. New York: Vintage Books, 1986.

Fort Caroline. Brochure printed by the Government Printing Office for distribution by the National Park service, GPO: 1984-609/10004.

Fort Clinch. Interpretive booklet printed by the Florida Department of Natural Resources for distribution by the Florida Division of Recreation and Parks, Tallahassee, FL, May 1982.

Fort Clinch State Park. Brochure printed by the Florida Department of Natural Resources for distribution by the Division of Recreation and Parks, Tallahassee, FL, September 1982.

Fort Foster Historic Site. Pamphlet printed by the Florida Department of Natural Resources for distribution by the Division of Recreation and Parks, Tallahassee, FL, July 1987.

Fort Gadsden State Historic Site. Pamphlet printed by the Florida Department of Natural Resources for distribution by the Division of Recreation and Parks, Tallahassee, FL, January 1982.

Fort Matanzas. Brochure printed by the Government Printing Office for distribution by the National Park Service, GPO: 1975-585-440/102.

The Fort Matanzas Stabilization Team (Luis Arana, Edwin Bearss, Randall Copeland, Gary Cummins, C. Craig Frazier, John Paige, George Schesventer and Terry Wong). Fort Matanzas National Monument Historic Structure Report, Fort Matanzas, St. Johns County, FL, November 1980 (document obtained from Denver Technical Information Center, D-1677).

Fort Mose, Historic State Park: African American Community of Freedom. Brochure printed and distributed by the Florida Park Service.

Gadsden, Captain James. "The Defenses of the Floridas: A Report of Captain James Gadsden, Aide-de-Camp to General Andrew Jackson." Edited by Mark F. Boyd. *Florida Historical Quarterly* XV, no.4 (April 1937).

Goza, William M. "The Fort King Road—1963." *Florida Historical Quarterly* XLIII, no. 1 (July 1964).

Gray, James M. *Florida Forts*. Lutz, FL: private publication, 1972.

Griffin, John W. "An Archeologist at Fort Gadsden." *Florida Historical Quarterly* XXVIII, no.4 (April 1950).

Grismer, Karl H. *The Story of Fort Myers*. St. Petersburg: St. Petersburg Printing Company, Inc., 1949.

Haas, Irvin. *Citadels, Ramparts and Stockades*. New York: Everest House, 1979.

Hawes, Leland. "Disease plagued fort during 2nd Seminole War." *Tampa Tribune*, December 4, 1988, history/heritage section.

———. "Lieutenant's letters tell of Fort Foster in 1830s." *Tampa Tribune*, December 4, 1988, history/heritage section.

Hill, Judy, "Let It Shine: Modernization will put Lighthouse on Automatic." *Tampa Tribune*, August 18, 1987, baylife section.

Huettel, Steve. "In Retreat." *Tampa Tribune*, November 28, 1993, nation/world section.

Interpretive Prospectus: Fort Caroline National Memorial, Park General Planning Reports, document number D-812A, Department of the Interior, July 1984 (document obtained from Denver Service Center of the National Park Service).

Jahoda, Gloria. *Florida: A History*. New York: W.W. Norton & Company, 1984.

Johns, John E. *Florida During the Civil War*. Gainesville: University of Florida Press, 1963.

Johnson, Karen. "Egmont Key, An Island Paradox." *Tampa Bay Magazine*, November–December 1994.

Kemp, Roy, (park manager of Fort Clinch State Park) to author, March 16, 1989, regarding specific information on the fort's armaments and about the fort's Spanish-American War battery.

Knetsch, Joe. *Florida's Seminole Wars, 1817–1858*. Charleston, SC: Arcadia Publishing, 2003.

Laumer, Frank. "This Was Fort Dade." *Florida Historical Quarterly* XLV, no. 1 (July 1966).

Lewis, Emanuel R. *Seacoast Fortifications of the United States*. Annapolis, MD: Leeward Publications Inc., 1979.

Marban, Jorge A. *Florida: Five Centuries of Hispanic History*. Miami: Ediciones Universal, 1979.

Miller, Janice Borton. *Juan de Quesada: Governor of Spanish East Florida 1790–1795*. Washington, D.C.: University Press of America, Inc., 1981.

Mormino, Gary R. "GI Joe Meets Jim Crow: Racial Violence and Reform in World War II Florida." *Florida Historical Quarterly* LXXIII, no. 1 (July 1994): 23–42.

Morris, Allen. *Florida Place Names*. Coral Gables, FL: University of Miami Press, 1974.

O'Toole, G.J.A. *The Spanish War: An American Epic 1898*. New York: W.W. Norton & Company, 1984.

Ott, Eloise Robinson, and Louis Hickman Chazal. *Ocali Country: Kingdom of the Sun*. Ocala, FL: Marion Publishers, Inc., 1966.

Parsons, Jeffery L. Fort Barrancas and Water Battery. Guide pamphlet published by the Eastern National Park and Monument Association.

Pittman, R.E. "Apalache During the British Occupation." Edited by Mark F. Boyd. *Florida Historical Quarterly* XII, no.3 (January 1934).

Potter, Woodburne. *The War in Florida*. Readex Microprint Corporation, 1966. Reprint of the 1836 edition.

Roberts, Robert B. *Encyclopedia of Historic Forts*. New York: Macmillan Publishing Company, 1988.

Sarles, Frank B. Historic Sites Report on Fort DeSoto, Pinellas County, FL. National Survey of Historic Sites and Buildings report done for the United States Department of the Interior (National Park Service), February 1960 (document obtained from the Denver Technical Service, document number D-5, DeSoto National Memorial Site file).

Schene, Michael. "Fort Foster: A Second Seminole War Fort." *Florida Historical Quarterly* LIV, no.3 (January 1976).

Tebeau, Charlton W. *A History of Florida*. Coral Gables: University of Miami Press, 1971.

Ward, James Robertson. *Old Hickory's Town*. Jacksonville: Old Hickory's Town, Incorporated, 1985.

Wares, Donna. "Tampa Bay Wildlife Refuges: Inhabitants Compete with Man for Survival." *Evening Independent*, July 30, 1983, mid-Pinellas edition.

Weaver, John R. *A Legacy in Brick and Stone: American Coastal Defense Forts of the Third System, 1816– 1867*. Missoula, MT: Pictorial Histories Publishing Company, 2001.

Wenhold, Lucy L. "The First Fort of San Marcos de Apalache." *Florida Historical Quarterly* XXXIV, no.4 (April 1956).

Wynne, Lewis N., and Robert A. Taylor. *Florida in the Civil War*. Charleston, SC: Arcadia Publishing, 2001.

Young, Rogers W. "The Transfer of Fort San Marcos and East Florida to the United States." *Florida Historical Quarterly* XIV, no.4 (April 1936).

Printed in the USA
CPSIA information can be obtained
at www.ICGtesting.com
LVHW080236041023
759906LV00021B/48